THEATRE SYMPOSIUM
A PUBLICATION OF THE SOUTHEASTERN THEATRE CONFERENCE

Theatre and Violence

Volume 7

Published by the

Southeastern Theatre Conference and

The University of Alabama Press

THEATRE SYMPOSIUM is published annually by the Southeastern Theatre Conference, Inc. (SETC), and by The University of Alabama Press. SETC nonstudent members receive the journal as a part of their membership under rules determined by SETC. For information on membership, write to SETC, P.O. Box 9868, Greensboro, NC 27429-0868. All other inquiries regarding subscriptions, circulation, purchase of individual copies, and requests to reprint materials should be addressed to The University of Alabama Press, Box 870380, Tuscaloosa, AL 35487-0380.

THEATRE SYMPOSIUM publishes works of scholarship resulting from a single-topic meeting held on a southeastern university campus each spring. A call for papers to be presented at that meeting is widely publicized each autumn for the following spring. Authors are therefore not encouraged to send unsolicited manuscripts directly to the editor. Information about the next symposium is available from the editor, John W. Frick, Department of Drama, University of Virginia, Culbreth Theatre, Charlottesville, VA 22903.

THEATRE SYMPOSIUM
A PUBLICATION OF THE SOUTHEASTERN THEATRE CONFERENCE

Volume 7 Contents *1999*

Introduction

SHORTLY AFTER NOON on Tuesday, 24 March, just ten days before the opening of the Symposium on Theatre and Violence held at the University of Virginia 2–4 April, two young boys (ages thirteen and eleven) armed with high-powered hunting rifles ambushed and killed four of their classmates and a teacher at a Jonesboro, Arkansas, middle school. Within the hour the tragedy had begun to be "mediatized," as network commentators interviewed law enforcement personnel and witnesses, and camera crews shot the grim remains of the slaughter—a sweater on the grass, an abandoned book bag, a lunch box, pools of blood on a sidewalk. And by the evening news the pundits had already begun to ask the "tough," analytical questions: What prompted the boys to do it? What had influenced their thought? Why didn't their moral code(s) prohibit such an action? What role did the media play in their attitudes toward violence? The symposium took place in the shadow of this massacre, and even though the events at Jonesboro were never once mentioned during the conference, the discourse and debate during the three days in Charlottesville was necessarily "framed" by this and similar tragedies and the prevalence of violence in our culture.

The conference was not an attempt to offer solutions to the problem of cultural violence but rather an effort to understand the nature of "represented" violence and then perhaps to begin to comprehend the theatre's role(s) and/or complicity in a culture of violence (or, at best, a culture that tolerates violence). In this regard anthropologist Nancy Scheper-Hughes's introductory article examines violence as an all-too-prevalent cultural phenomenon. In the second section of the journal, *Rhetorical and Historical Perspectives,* Andrea Nouryeh, Lesley Ferris,

James Harley, and John Countryman and Charlotte Headrick explore violence as an integral element in both dramatic texts and performance throughout the history of the theatre. The third section features articles dealing with various facets of the actual staging of violence written by Fight Masters Joseph Martinez and Dale Girard and Fight Director Colleen Kelly, all members of the Society of American Fight Directors. In the final section William Boles, Jane Barnette, and Leslie Wade analyze contemporary examples of theatrical violence that exist at the fringes of social acceptability.

Of the eleven articles contained in this volume, four (authored by Professors Scheper-Hughes, Ferris, Martinez, and Girard) originated as keynote presentations at the April symposium; the seven remaining articles were selected by members of the editorial board, serving as jury, from the twenty-two papers presented at the conference.

I wish to thank the University of Virginia Department of Drama and the Virginia Foundation for the Humanities Institute for Violence, Culture and Survival for their support of the conference and the editorial board and staff for their work on this volume. I am especially indebted to former editors Phil Hill and Stanley Longman for their advice and support.

JOHN W. FRICK
Editor

Sacred Wounds

Making Sense of Violence

Nancy Scheper-Hughes

Coming to Our Senses: Anthropology and Violence

VIOLENCE IS HARDLY a natural subject for the anthropologist. In fact, everything in our training, in our disposition, predisposes us not to see the political or implicit, everyday, structural violence that distorts and maims the lives of our subjects. Our particular moral sensibility orients us toward "positive" cultural norms rather than toward deviance, to consent and consensus rather than to conflict and dissent.

There has been a long and honorable tradition in anthropology of not studying violence. Our literature on warfare—"primitive" or "civilized" as the case may be, but equally savage in each instance—is small. Our contribution to understanding all levels of violence—from domestic and sexual abuse to the culturally imposed tortures of adult male circumcision (as practiced among urban Xhosa young men with whom I have been working) or female circumcision and infibulation, to individual homicides, to state-sponsored terrorism, to "dirty" wars, and genocide—is likewise extremely modest. The neglect of violence is dictated by "honorable" concerns, especially the long-standing anthropological commitment to see the good, the right, and the just in those third-world societies so often misjudged in terms of Eurocentric and ethnocentric aims and values. A basic premise guiding anthropological fieldwork has been to see, hear, and report no evil (and little violence).

In his memoir, *After the Fact*, master ethnographer Clifford Geertz (1995) notes wryly that he always had the uncomfortable feeling of having arrived too early or too late to catch the huge political events and violent upheavals in his respective field sites in Morocco and Java. But later in the memoir, he notes that he consciously (and understandably) avoided the political conflicts by moving back and forth between his field sites during relative periods of calm. Orin Starn refers to this common anthropological phenomenon as "missing the revolution" (1992). Unless we are to intuit some deeper political significance to Geertz's studied attention to the semiotics of the Balinese cock fight, there is nothing in his elegant ethnographies hinting at the killing fields—the massacre of suspected Communist insurgents by Islamic fundamentalists in 1965, which rivaled recent events in Rwanda for ferocity—that began to engulf Java soon after the anthropologist had departed.

But the world, the objects of our study, and the uses of anthropology have changed considerably. Those of us who are privileged to observe human events close up and over time and who are privy to local, community, and even at times to state secrets that are generally hidden from view until much later—after the collective graves have been discovered and the body counts made—are beginning to recognize another ethical position: the naming and the identification of the sources, structures, and institutions of violence that were once "protected" by the anthropological stance of cultural, moral, and political relativism.

Consequently, there has been a good deal of rethinking our relations to our subjects. Claude Lévi-Strauss (1995), fast approaching the end of his long and distinguished career, opened his recently published photographic memoir, *Saudades do Brasil* (Homesickness for Brazil), with a sobering caveat. He warned the reader that the lyrically beautiful images of "pristine" rain forest Brazilian Indians about to be presented—photos he took between 1935 and 1939 in the interior of Brazil—should not be trusted. The images were illusory, he cautioned. The world they portray no longer exists. The starkly beautiful, seemingly timeless Nambikwara, Caduveo, and Bororo Indians captured in his photos bear no resemblance to the reduced populations one might find today camped out by the sides of busy truck routes or loitering in urban villages that look like slums carved out of a gutted wilderness. The Nambikwara and their Amerindian neighbors have been decimated and reduced by wage labor, gold prospecting, prostitution, and the diseases of cultural and sexual contact: smallpox, TB, AIDS, syphilis.

But the old master's confession went even further. His early photos, which captured simple, naked Indians sleeping on the ground under seemingly romantic shelters of palm leaves, have nothing to do with a state of pristine, "primitive humanity" that has since been lost. The photos already show the effects of a savage European colonization on the once culturally rich, highly developed, and populous civilizations of central Brazil and the Amazon. Following contact with the European conquerors, the indigenous Brazilian civilizations were destroyed, leaving behind only sad remnants of themselves, a people not so much "primitive" as "stranded" and stripped of their material and symbolic wealth. What Lévi-Strauss's camera had captured were the casualties of a particularly violent kind of human strip mining, an invisible genocide, the magnitude of which the anthropologist was, at the time, naively unaware.

I implicate myself as well in this anthropological scenario, for it took me more than two decades to confront the question of overt political violence, which, given my choice of early field sites—Ireland in the mid-1970s and Brazil during the worst of the military state years—required a massive dose of denial. While studying the madness of everyday life in the mid-1970s in a small, quiet peasant community in western Ireland, I was largely concerned with interior spaces, with the small dark psychodramas of scapegoating and labeling within traditional farm households that were driving so many young bachelors to drink and to bouts of depression and schizophrenia. I paid scant attention to the mundane political activities of little Matty Dowd, from whom we rented our cottage in the mountain hamlet of Ballynalacken and who used our attic to store a small arsenal of guns and explosives that he and a few of his Sinn Fein buddies were running to Northern Ireland. Consequently, I left unexamined the possible links between the political violence in Northern Ireland and the tortured family dramas in West Kerry that I carefully documented and which certainly had a violence of their own.

Since then, I have continued to study other forms of "everyday" violence: the abuses of medicine and psychiatry practiced in bad faith against the weak, the mad, and the hungry including, most recently, the abuses of the bodies of the socially disadvantaged in transplant surgery (see Scheper-Hughes 1998); and the social indifference to child death in northeast Brazil that allowed political leaders, priests, coffin makers, and shantytown mothers to dispatch a multitude of hungry "angel-babies" to the afterlife. But even in Brazil I did not begin to study state and political violence until, beginning in the late 1980s, the half-grown sons of some of my friends and neighbors in the shantytown of Alto do Cruzeiro began to "disappear," their mutilated bodies turning up later, the handiwork of police-infiltrated local death squads.

Until then I had believed that the analysis of political violence occurring in the context of military dictatorships and police states, in times of transition during and after civil wars and wars of liberation, was best handled by journalists. Anthropologists were too slow, too hesitant, too reflective, and our knowledge was too local and too embedded to keep pace with political events, which were altogether too fast and unstable. Consequently, by the time we had something to say, it was usually obsolete. But as the Brazilian newspapers insisted on running stories about the "dangerousness" and the "violence" of shantytown dwellers—especially of poor young black men and boys, a perceived threat that made the work of the death squads seem like a necessary defense against the anarchy of the favela—I saw that anthropological interventions were needed to correct the manipulative half-truths of the media. Our anthropological truths might be false or partial, but they were certainly less false than those of the media.

Everyday Violence

Here I want to forge a link between my earlier concerns with everyday, familiar, routinized violence and state and macrolevel political violence. My remarks will revisit a key theme in my work that is derived from a radical tradition of social science: a concern with the popular consent to "everyday violence" that makes possible a consent to militarism, dirty wars, and even genocide. By "everyday violence" I mean the implicit, legitimate, organized, and routinized violence of particular social, political, and state formations. This kind of violence is related to, but distinct from, Pierre Bourdieu's (1977; 1996) notion of "symbolic violence" and is closest to what Taussig (1989), citing Benjamin, calls "terror as usual."

Bourdieu finds aggression, domination, and violence in the least likely places—in the architecture of the home, in the tense exchange of gifts, in systems of kinship classification, in all the various uses of culture. Violence, Bourdieu suggests, is everywhere in social practice. It is "misrecognized" because its very familiarity renders it invisible. Along with Gramsci, Foucault, Sartre, and other modern theorists of power and domination, Bourdieu treats direct physical violence as a crude, uneconomical, and unnecessary mode of domination. It is less efficient and, following Arendt (1969), it is certainly less legitimate. The Foucauldian narrative (*Discipline and Punish* [1979], for example) suggests that during the past two hundred years, torture as a legitimate tool of the state officially disappeared in civilized countries. More refined methods for extracting consent were developed and implemented by modern "technicians of the social consensus," including labor and management specialists, urban planners, entertainment and media technicians, educators and, of course, doctors, counselors, psychiatrists, and social workers.

Contrary to the expectations of the "gloved hands of the state" theorists, at the close of the twentieth century we are witnessing a repugnant resurgence of the political uses of graphic, physical torture. And we are seeing some new twists in the modernization of torture. In South America, for example, during the 1970s and 1980s, state torture was primarily preventative—a political inoculation meant to nip contaminating ideas and practices in the bud. In Argentina, Chile, Uruguay, and Brazil, persons being detained, tortured, and killed usually had nothing to confess except their unwillingness and refusal to be killed (Weschler 1990). This highly organized form of state violence was carried out to obtain total and unconditional consent. In the new logic of the hypermodern state, crude violence is apparently once again free to reveal itself for what it is.

Anthropologists have finally begun to address the shocking rebirth of late-twentieth-century genocide in Africa (Mallki 1996), South Asia (V. Das 1997; V. Daniel 1997) and Central Europe (Olujic 1998). These anthropologists have witnessed in their own field sites the recurrence of what we thought could never happen again. Consequently, I have returned to the questions that so vexed a generation of post-Holocaust social theorists: What makes genocide possible? How shall we explain the alarming complicity of otherwise "ordinary" and "good" people in outbreaks of radical violence perpetrated by the state, police, military, and ethnic groups?

Adorno and his Frankfurt School colleagues (see Geuss 1981) have suggested that the seemingly willing participation of ordinary people in genocidal acts requires strong childhood conditioning in mindless obedience to authority figures, in addition to powerful ideologies, such as anti-Semitism. But Goldhagen (1996), relying on compelling testimony, has argued that millions of ordinary Germans participated willingly, even eagerly, in the Holocaust, not for fear of the authorities but because of race hatred alone. Alternatively, I have suggested a kind of genocidal continuum, made up of a multitude of what I have elsewhere called "small wars and invisible genocides" (see Scheper-Hughes 1996, 1997) conducted in the normative, ordinary social spaces of public schools, clinics, emergency rooms, hospital charity wards, nursing homes, city halls, court rooms, prisons, detention centers, and public morgues.

The capacity of humans to reduce other humans to nonpersons, to things, has motivated much of my anthropological work on the structures, meanings, and practices of "everyday violence." We must recognize in our species and in ourselves a genocidal capacity and exercise a defensive hypervigilance and hypersensitivity to less-dramatic, less-visible, permitted, and far more common acts of "structural" violence, by which I mean all expressions of social exclusion, dehumanization, depersonalization, pseudo-speciation, and reification that normalize the atrocious and the otherwise unthinkable. Perhaps this self-mobilization for constant shock and a state of hyperarousal are "natural" responses to Walter Benjamin's view of modern history as a chronic "state of emergency" (1969, 253).

In referring to "small wars and invisible genocides," I know that I am walking on thin ice. My suggestion of a "genocidal continuum" flies in the face of a tradition within genocide studies (see, for example, Fackenheim 1970) that argues for the absolute uniqueness of the Jewish Holocaust. Yet I do make such comparisons between the Holocaust and other less-visible (because normative) acts of violence, though I proceed cautiously, joining others who have called attention to forms and spaces of previously unrecognized, gratuitous, and useless social suffering (Levinas 1986; Kleinman and Kleinman 1997). If there is a moral and political risk in extending as powerful a metaphor as "genocide" into spaces where we might not have previously seen it, the benefit lies in sensitizing people to genocidal-like practices and sentiments that are daily enacted as normative behavior by ordinary citizens.

Hannah Arendt (1963) paved the way in recognizing the potential within otherwise decent people to become dedicated technicians of genocide under particular social and historical conditions. In this regard Bourdieu's partial and unfinished theory of violence is useful. By including the softer, symbolic forms of violence hidden in the minutia of "normal" social practices, Bourdieu forces us to reconsider the broader meanings and status of violence, especially the links between "everyday violence" and more explicit political terror.

I, however, prefer the late Italian phenomenologist and later Marxist psychiatrist Franco Basaglia's (1986) suggestive though under-theorized notion of "peace-time crimes" *(crimini di pace)* because it imagines a more direct relationship between war crimes and peace crimes. Basaglia grasped a continuity between extraordinary and ordinary violence, between the everyday forms and institutions of implicit violence and the explicit atrocities of wartime. Peacetime crimes suggest that war crimes are quite ordinary, everyday crimes of public consent that are applied systematically and dramatically in times of war. Consider the parallel uses and meanings of rape during peacetime and wartime or the resemblances between public consent to everyday border raids and physical assaults by INS agents on Mexican aliens and the state-sponsored genocide of the historical Cherokee Indians' "Trail of Tears."

Alternatively, peacetime crimes suggest that everyday forms of state violence make possible a certain kind of national, domestic "peace." Internal "stability" is purchased with the currency of peacetime crimes. For example, how many public executions of run-of-the-mill, lower-class ne'er-do-wells are needed in the populous states of Texas, Louisiana, and California to make life feel more secure for the affluent? How many new and improved prisons do we need to build in the United States to contain an expanding population of young black men cast as "public enemies"? Are we satisfied with a 10 percent confinement rate? A 20 percent confinement rate? More still? What can it possibly mean when jails have become a "normative" socializing experience for a whole category of young people? Ordinary peacetime crimes—such as the steady evolution of American prisons into alternative black concentration camps—are among the "small wars and invisible genocides" to which I refer. They are invisible not because they are secreted away or hidden from view but quite the opposite. As Wittgenstein observed, the things that are hardest to perceive are those that are right before our eyes and therefore taken for granted (Wittgenstein, cited in Sacks 42).

Franco Basaglia's own awakening happened when he first entered an Italian manicomio (a traditional state mental asylum) as a psychiatric intern after World War II. He was immediately struck by a frightening sense of déjà vu—the odor of defecation, sweat, and death catapulted him back to the prison cell where he had been held as a member of the Italian Resistance during the German occupation. That single, terrifying moment became the basis for his equation of mental hospitals with concentration camps and the links between war crimes and peacetime crimes.

International war tribunals had just been established to try those guilty of war crimes, which, for the first time, were treated as crimes against humanity. Meanwhile, Dr. Basaglia struggled to unmask the invisible, still unrecognized, crimes against humanity practiced in Italian state mental asylums after the war. The supreme irony was that some of the more disturbed inmates were already suffering from war-related post-traumatic stress disorders only to encounter in the hospital another battery of medically sanctioned tortures, including the all-too-familiar applications of solitary confinement; physical restraint; removal of clothing; exposure to cold, dirt, and sleep deprivation, and professionally applied "strangle-holds."[1]

---

[1] Indeed, the human repertoire of body and soul wounding techniques are pathetically repetitive and unimaginative, as I have just learned during my recent stay in South Africa, where during February and March 1998 I observed South Africa's Truth and Reconciliation Commission Hearings. Former members of South Africa's apartheid police and security forces described in painful detail the banal but savage techniques of torture that they used "to break" ANC comrades, whom they persist to this day to refer to as "terrorists."

As new director of the state mental asylum at Gorizia, Basaglia began to reverse the regime and culture of terror that had masqueraded as therapy and that had contributed to the premature deaths of hospital inmates. He used elements of guerrilla theatre, drama, surprise, and the therapeutics of the absurd to contest and undo the psychic damage of the asylum. Believing that it was impossible to "reform" a system that had turned long-term mental patients into "grateful" slaves, Dr. Basaglia did the unthinkable: He embarked with his patients on a project of "destroying" and "negating" the institution. He tried to engage the patients' long-buried aggressivity, which he saw as a positive healing force. Although everything in the traditional asylum was mobilized to prevent "patient aggression" and "destructiveness," Basaglia believed that it was the long-term inmate's paralyzing passivity that was the most obdurate and crippling sign of illness.

Asylum patients had been wards of a medical police state for so long that they had come to accept their condition of confinement and exclusion as natural and inevitable; so when Dr. Basaglia unlocked the doors of the isolation cells in which some of the more "violent" patients had been contained, the inmates just sat there, patiently waiting to be told what to do next. The mental hospital, Basaglia concluded, was a prison, a primary institution of social and political violence, and he recruited even the most regressed and "backward" patients in the project of "destroying" the institution and its exclusionary logic. Keys, locks, and straight jackets were thrown away; filthy, torn bed linens were thrown out of windows; bars and barbed wire were removed. Tearing down a foul and deteriorated back ward became a patient self-help project. If a patient was released back into the community, his or her bed was taken away as a sign that no other unfortunate person should ever again occupy that "liberated" space. The patients galvanized around a key symbol, the construction in the hospital yard at Gorizia of a huge, papier-mâché horse, Marco Cavalho, which they paraded throughout the city as a public statement of their awakening and liberation.

Resistance to the project of "democratic psychiatry" came from predictable quarters—the families of especially older patients, who did not want to deal with their "crazy" relations, and the nurses and orderlies who had had the most physical contact with the inmates and who were most invested in the regime of violent control. Dr. Basaglia recognized the suffering of families, and his team sought to create alternative, safe, yet permissive forms of state-supported housing for liberated patients. He worked closely with the nurses, helping them to discover their own class links to the public mental patients. Together, doctors and nurses explored a new role—that of the "negative" intellectual who turns against the violent, bureaucratic institution that provides him or her with a livelihood in order to forge a new solidarity with the patient.

The analogic thinking that enabled Franco Basaglia to perceive the logical relations between concentration camps and mental hospitals, between "war crimes" and "peacetime crimes," between prisoners and mental patients allowed him to see the willingness of ordinary people (Basaglia's "practical technicians") to enforce, sometimes with gusto, "genocidal-like" crimes against types of people thought of as mere waste, as rubbish, as altogether deficient in humanity, and ultimately as "better off dead." Historically, the mad and the mentally deficient have often fallen into this category, as have the very old and the pauperized, the sick-poor, as well as a great many women and children. Erik Erikson has labeled this "pseudo-speciation," by which he meant the human tendency to classify some individuals or social groups as less than fully human.

Street Children as Vermin

Although Latin Americans—and Brazilians in particular—are known for their love of children, they do not love so-called street children, who have multiplied in great numbers following the transitions to open-market, neoliberal economies and to more democratic structures. Suddenly—or so it has seemed to a great many people in post-military, police-state Brazil, Venezuela, and Guatemala—favelas, shantytowns, and poor barrios ruptured, and "homeless" and "dirty" street children seemed to be everywhere, displaying their "criminal" needs. Democratization itself provoked a crisis of security, and ordinary citizens looked increasingly to vigilantes to provide the "dirty work" of clearing the streets of paupers and marginals now thought of as enemies of the new, neoliberal states.

In Brazil my recent studies have focused on police and death-squad attacks on older street children, who are often described as "dirty vermin," so that metaphors of "street cleaning," "trash removal," "fly swatting," "pest removal," and "urban hygiene" have been invoked to garner broad-based public support for police and death-squad activities (such as the infamous Candaleria massacre, in which off-duty policemen fired into a huddle of two dozen sleeping street children, killing eight of them and seriously wounding many others). Even the term "street child" represents a kind of symbolic apartheid as urban space has become increasingly "privatized." As long as poor, "dirty" street children are contained in the slum, the favela, or where they belong, they are not viewed as an urgent social problem about which something must be done.

The real issue is the preoccupation of one social class with the "proper place" of another social class. Like dirt, which is acceptable when it is in the yard but not when it is found under the nails, "dirty" street children are simply children "out of place." In Brazil "street" and "home" designate more than social space; they are moral entities, spheres of social action, and ethical provinces. Home is the realm of relational ties and privilege that confer social personhood, human rights, and full citizenship. Street is an unbounded and dangerous realm, the space of the "masses" (*o povo*), where one can be treated anonymously. Rights belong to the realm of the home. Street children, typically barefoot, shirtless, and unattached to a home, represent the extremes of social marginality and anonymity. They occupy a particularly degraded social position within the Brazilian hierarchy of place and power. As denizens of the street, these semiautonomous kids are separated from all that can confer relationship and propriety, without which rights and citizenship are impossible.

I have been following a cohort of some forty semiautonomous, mostly homeless street kids in the interior market town of Bom Jesus in Pernambuco. My study began informally in 1982 with a cohort of children four to twelve years old who attached themselves to our household, and it continued through the summer of 1997. Twenty-two of the original cohort are dead, killed by police in acts of what are designated "legitimate homicides." Others disappeared and remain missing; still others are in jail. Some of these have already become killers, recruited by older "intermediaries" (some with ties not only to local police but to corrupt judges and to local merchants) as hired guns in "death squad" murders of other street children. And so the cycle of violence turns, with children killing children, egged on by the so-called forces of state law and order themselves.

Rubbish People

In this country we need go no further than our own medical clinics, emergency rooms, public hospitals, and old age homes to encounter other classes of "rubbish people" treated with as much indifference and malevolence as mental patients in the traditional Italian *manicomio* or street kids in South America. My experience with nursing homes is personal and extremely painful. Ever-increasing numbers of the aged are both sick and poor because of the astronomical cost of late-life medical care. These elderly are at risk of spending their remaining time in public or less-expensive private institutions for the aged, like "Happy Valley," where the care of residents is delegated to grossly underpaid and undertrained workers. The workers protect themselves by turning the persons and bodies under their protection into things, bulky objects that can be dealt with in shorter and shorter intervals. Economic pressures are strong and bear down on the "staffers" to minimize the personal care and attention given to the residents, especially those whose limited savings have already been used up by the institution and who are now supported by the state on Medicare.

The underpaid staff need to duck away as often as possible, for a smoke, a snack, or a breath of air; but other work survival tactics are less defensible. The personal names of residents are dropped and they are often addressed as "you," instead of by name, or no account is taken of expressed wishes, so that sooner or later any requests or expressions of personal preference—to turn the heat up or down, to open or close the window, to bring a cold drink, to lower the volume on the TV or change a channel—are extinguished. Passivity sets in. When the body is rolled from one side or the other for cleaning or to clean the sheets (body and sheets are equated); when the resident is wheeled conveniently into a corner so that the floor can be more easily mopped; when cleaning staff do little to suppress expressions of disgust at urine, feces, or phlegm out of place—on clothing, under the nails, on wheelchairs, or in wastepaper baskets—those persons trapped inside failing bodies may also come to see themselves as "dirty," "vile," "disgusting," as objects or as nonpersons. An essay by Jules Henry (1966) on "Hospitals for the Aged Poor," which documents the attack on the elderly individual's dwindling stock of personal and psychological "capital" by unconscious hospital and nursing-home staff, is as true today as when it was first written.

The institutional destruction of personhood is aided by the material circumstances of the nursing home. When all personal objects—toothbrush, comb, glasses, towels, pens, and pencils—continue to disappear no matter how many times they have been replaced, the resident (if he or she knows what is good for him or her) finally accepts the situation and adapts in other ways. Eventually, residents are compelled to use other objects, which are more available, for purposes for which they were never intended. The plastic wastepaper basket becomes the urinal, the urinal the wash basin; the water glass becomes a spittoon; the hated adult diaper is used defiantly as a table napkin; and so forth. Meanwhile, the institutional violence and indifference are masked as the resident's own state of mental confusion and incompetence. And everything in the nature of the institution invites the resident to further regression, to give up, to accept his or her inevitable and less-than-human status. But where are the forces of liberation or a movement analogous to Basaglia's "Democratic Psychiatry?"

Acceptable Death

Denial is a prerequisite of dehumanization, violence, and genocide. In *Death without Weeping* (1992), I explored the normalization and social indifference to staggering infant and child mortality in shantytown favelas of northeast Brazil. Local political leaders, Catholic priests and nuns, coffin makers, and shantytown mothers themselves casually dispatched a multitude of hungry "angel-babies" to the afterlife each year saying, "Well, they themselves wanted to die." The babies were described as having no "taste," no "knack," no "talent" for life.

Medical practices, such as prescribing powerful tranquilizers to fretful and frightfully hungry babies, Catholic ritual celebrations of the death of "angel-babies," and the bureaucratic indifference of political leaders who dispensed free baby coffins but no food to hungry families and children interacted with maternal practices such as radically reducing food and liquids to severely malnourished and dehydrated babies to help them (their mothers said) die quickly and well. Perceived as already "doomed," sickly infants were described as less than human creatures, as ghostly angel-babies, inhabiting a terrain midway between life and death. "Really and truly," mothers said, "it is better that these spirit-children return to where they came from."

The ability of economically threatened women to help those infants who, they said, "needed to die" required an existential "letting go" (in contrast to the maternal work of "holding on," holding close and holding dear). Letting go required a leap of faith that was not easy to achieve. "Holy indifference" in the face of adversity was a cherished but elusive value for these desperately poor Catholic women, who sometimes said that infants died, like Jesus, so that others, especially themselves, could live.

The question that lingered was whether this Kierkegaardian "leap of faith" entailed a certain Marxist "bad faith" as well. I am not blaming shantytown mothers for putting their own and their older children's survival before that of their preconscious infants. These were overdetermined moral choices that no person should be forced to make. However, the "bad faith" to which I refer concerns the women's denial, their refusal to accept the authorship of their acts, and their willingness to project the deaths of their angel-babies onto the will and desire of the doomed infants themselves.

I gradually came to think of the shantytown angel-babies in terms of René Girard's (1987) idea of sacrificial violence and the ritual scape-goat. The given-up, given-up-on babies had been sacrificed in the face of terrible conflicts about scarcity and survival. It was here that peace-time and wartime, maternal thinking and military thinking, converged. When angels (or martyrs) are fashioned from the dead bodies of those who die young, "maternal thinking" most resembles military, especially wartime, thinking. On the battlefield, as in the shantytown, triage, thinking in sets, and a belief in the magical replaceability of the dead predominate.

Above all, ideas of "acceptable death" and of "meaningful," rather than useless, suffering extinguish rage and grief for those whose lives are taken and allow for the recruitment of new lives and new bodies into the struggle. Just as shantytown mothers in Brazil consoled each other that their hungry babies died because they were "meant" to die or because they "had" to die, Northern Irish mothers and South Afri-can township mothers console each other at political wakes and funerals during wartime and in times of political struggle with the belief that their sacrificed and "martyred" children died purposefully and died well. This kind of thinking is not exclusive to any particular class of people. Whenever we allow ourselves to attribute some meaning, whether po-litical or spiritual, to the useless suffering of others, we behave a bit like public executioners, a theme to which I will now turn.

Making Sense of Suffering and Violence

Anthropology is about meaning, about making sense, in a world that has become increasingly absurd. When the subject is violence and indi-vidual or collective suffering, however, our task becomes morally am-biguous, as I will illustrate with a few graphic scenes from my recent re-search on political violence and reconciliation in the New South Africa.

I went to the Cape of Good Hope in 1993 to lose myself in a new anthropological field site following the publication of *Death without Weeping: The Violence of Everyday Life in Brazil* (1992), which concluded more than a decade of ethnographic research on love and death in the impoverished sugar plantations of northeast Brazil. I had gone to South Africa to be where something good, beautiful, and hopeful was about to happen. But the approaching democratic elections that would sweep Mr. Mandela and the African National Congress (ANC) to power in a glorious display of popular victory were preceded by a final, desperate attempt of the National Party government's internal security and de-fense forces to disrupt the transition.

Meanwhile, the PAC (Pan African Congress), APLA (Azanian

People's Liberation Army), and other revolutionary groups, divided over the terms of the negotiated settlement being hammered out in Kempton Park, held out for the duration of the militant struggle. Consequently, 1993–94 turned into the worst year of political violence and deaths in more than a decade of undeclared civil war.

In July 1993, the day after my family and I arrived in Cape Town, three young men dressed in overalls and head scarves burst into the evening service of St. James Evangelical Christian Church in the white suburb of Kenilworth, bordering the University of Cape Town community where we had just settled into a small flat. The men opened up with several rounds of ammunition and tossed nail-spiked hand grenades into the congregation of more than four hundred worshipers while they were singing the hymn, "Come to the Garden." In seconds eleven people were dead and more than fifty others seriously wounded and maimed. More might have died in the St. James Massacre, as it later came to be called, had not a young man seated at the back of the church pulled out a revolver and returned fire on the assailants, who fled from the Church and escaped in a getaway car that had been stolen earlier that day in Khayelitsha, a sprawling black township containing nearly a million "refugees" from the former apartheid designated homelands.

Barely a month later, during an antigovernment strike called "Operation Barcelona," American Fulbright student, Amy Biehl, was dragged from her car in Guguletu township in Cape Town and stoned to death by a jeering mob of radicalized students. The high school student ringleaders identified Amy as a white person, and therefore as an "agent" of the state, a hated enemy "settler." The next day, following a memorial ceremony at the University of the Western Cape, representatives of the ANC Women's League asked for volunteers, especially white women, to march into Guguletu township to assemble at the spot where Amy Biehl was killed in an effort to "take back the township" so that there would be no more "No Go" Zones for blacks, whites or coloreds in the new nonracist South Africa. Here, I quote from my field notes regarding the incident that contributed to the ironic title of this article, "Making Sense of Violence":

> At the bridge leading into Guguletu some ANC people are distributing posters to carry into the township that is still reeling from the attack. Everyone in our silent and scared little crowd is being choosy. "Comrades Come in All Colors" is favored over "Farewell Amy" written in Zulu which I got stuck with for a while. Guguletu is a Xhosa speaking township; no time for ecumenical sentiments today. So, I quickly discard that poster and pick up a seemingly innocuous one reading: "STOP THE SENSELESS

VIOLENCE," and I joined the long march from the Shoprite supermarket, over the bridge and through the squatter camp, across the highway leading into "Gugs." . . .

So here we are jump-dancing the militant Southern African toyi-toyi into "Gugs" less than 24 hours after Amy was dragged from her car and pummeled to death at a township gas station. We dance past silent young men with beer bottles in their hands who make unpleasant gestures. But I continue to flash my stupid, terrified grin holding the offending poster now in front of my white "settler" face, all the while second-guessing peoples' reactions to the thoughtless, senseless words for which I am now a poster girl.

Does senseless violence imply that the police are sensible in their attacks on the township? Is senseless yet another racist code for irrational Black violence as opposed to rational, sensible, everyday, structural white violence? What does "take back the townships" mean? From whom? By whom? By me of all people? What are we doing here? I know what my sensible, grown kids would say: "Go home, old lady! These folks don't want you there." Ah, but it's too late now for my sensible kids' advice.

So, I awkwardly toyi-toyi back and forth, forward and back, waiting for one of the surly young men to pull out a handgun and start shooting at my feet. Higher, Higher! Faster! Faster! My funky armpits aren't the only source of the pungent, anxious sweat that permeates the thickly polluted stale air. "Gugs" does not seem a friendly place. No one from the township joins our pathetic little parade. It is about a quarter of a mile to the Caltex gas station where, on a public road in full view of a row of cement block houses, Amy was attacked in broad daylight for carrying her Black comrades home. Why didn't anyone stop the attack? What was the source of their complicity? Fear? Indifference? Approval? Or is this what political resistance looks like when it's up in your face? (Field Notes, 25 August 1993).[2]

Then, on 30 December 1993 a tavern in the bohemian student quarter of Observatory was attacked by three PAC militants, and four people were killed. Two of them were students at the University of Cape Town; a third was a young, mixed-race schoolteacher; the fourth was an acquaintance of ours, the Portuguese-speaking owner of a seafood restaurant where we often went to "matar saudades" (kill our homesickness) for Brazil. Two of our three adult children were just a few doors away, celebrating the end of the year at another student hangout,

---

[2]Unless otherwise indicated, all directly cited observations were recorded by the author/anthropologist in her "field notes," which are the transcriptions (and analysis) of handwritten journal entries and audiotaped interviews collected "in the field." The field work for this article took place in 1993–94, the spring of 1996, and in the winter (January–February) of 1998.

Pancho's, when the tavern massacre took place. It was luck that had kept them from the pub where a popular black musician was playing that night. The memory of the four frozen and startled faces of the victims—for I accompanied the state pathologist to the Salt River Mortuary for the autopsies and painful identifications by family and friends—overdetermined the focus of my research on democracy and violence.

These much-publicized incidents of so called black-on-white violence were exceptions, of course, to the general rule of "white-on-black" structural and political violence, often carried out by paid or intimidated black collaborators. Because of my insertion into the still deeply racially segregated South African context as a visiting professor at the University of Cape Town (1993–1994), my direct "experience" of the violence was skewed toward the statistically, but not existentially, insignificant attacks by the apartheid government and by the revolutionary forces on white "targets." My attention to these particular and rare instances should not be taken as a negation of the rule of everyday, institutionalized, routinized, taken-for-granted violence against black South Africans.

In fact, so overwhelming and numbing were the daily statistics on black violent deaths that even the "liberal" white press and the black medium newspapers recorded them as un-named and dehumanized body counts: "Another 40 Bodies found on the East Rand"; "Dozen Bodies removed from Guguletu in Weekend Casualties"; "Nine Bodies found in two shacks gutted by fires in Khayelitsha"; "Charred bodies of seven people, including a 50 year old woman and her teenage daughter, found in Katlehong Railway Station on Friday"; "Unidentified Bodies Pile Up in Germiston Mortuary." Violent deaths were and remain the scourge of black South Africans. Despite their overwhelming preoccupation with it, white South Africans were almost completely insulated from, and miraculously spared, the political and criminal/anarchic violence that accompanied the democratic transition.

Of course, many beautiful things also happened during that excessively violent yet triumphal year. In the end the elections prevailed, and a celebratory mood bathed all South Africans in a sea of goodwill. A sense of humor and vitality emerged and even the intensely private, claustrophobic, worlds of long-hibernating white Capetonians opened a crack into a newly fashioned public space. Indeed, there was reason to celebrate in this land of terrible beauty.

The legacy of violence, however, remains. The scars are deep and etched into the gutted and destroyed landscapes left by the apartheid state, in the empty spaces left by those who died in the political violence, and in the wounded bodies of those who survived the violence but just barely. Again, I quote from my field notes:

> You cannot avoid them for they are present at every political event. Father Michael Lapsley with his startling, metal hooks where his hands should be. . . . There he is mischievously lighting a young woman's cigarette (a magician's trick!) or, over there, skillfully holding the stem of a wine glass raised in a defiant toast. . . . Once the shock leaves, one wants to caress his gentle hook-hands, to stroke the ruptured, permanently discolored skin where his right eye once was, and to toast him, noble wounded warrior, with wine goblets raised high, clinking glass with metal and champagne with tears. And over there, with his back carelessly turned to the door, stands Albie Sachs with his handsomely lined face and his resonant soothing voice, the agnostics' theologian, dressed in his priestly robes, his favorite bright and bold dashiki, waving his phantom limb, to make a point. That ever-present missing piece is Albie's most expressive body part and he gestures forcefully with the freely waving sleeve, his sweet banner of liberty. . . . Of thee, I sing, Albie. (Field Notes, 17 May 1994)

In recent years an anthropology of suffering has emerged as a new kind of theodicy, a cultural inquiry into the ways that people attempt to explain, account for, and justify the presence of pain, misfortune, affliction, evil in the world. At times of crisis, at moments of intense suffering, individuals demand an answer to the existential question: "Why me, oh God? Of all people? Why Now?" The quest for meaning may be poised to vindicate an indifferent God, to quell one's self-doubt, or to shore up one's faith in an orderly, just, and righteous world. The individual sufferer will construct a personal narrative with or without the help of doctors, priests, psychologists, or anthropologists. Evidently, the one thing humans seem unable to accept is the idea that the world may be deficient in meaning.

Ethical dilemmas enter the arena when people, including anthropologists, try to account for the suffering of the Other. This is magnified during or following an epidemic, a natural or a political disaster, or whenever tragedy hits the entire community. The existential "Why me?" often becomes the "Why Not Me?" "Why was I spared?" As survivors, humans, both individually and collectively, try to find some logic, some meaning, some purpose behind their exemption, their saving grace (see Bode 198).

Take, for example, the St. James congregation mentioned earlier. Although most congregation members were extremely faithful in their attendance, some regular worshipers did, of course, miss the Sunday service on that rainy evening in late July. A clerical worker in the medical school had car trouble; a secretary was down with the flu; a student grew impatient waiting in the rain for her best friend to arrive and went home rather than disrupt the service after it had begun. Each one shared with me their thoughts about why God had chosen to spare them on that night and their doubts about whether it was a good or a bad thing to have been spared the massacre. "You see, God was speaking to us very directly at the moment of the blast," said Marlene, expressing her chagrin at having missed the massacre.

A few days after the attack I joined a few dozen parishioners, most of them women, for the regular coffee klatch held after evening services in a Christian coffeehouse above the church. The parishioners' own interpretations of the meaning of the massacre were more mystical and more embodied than the distanced and intellectualized sermon their pastor, Bishop Frank Reteif, had just delivered. They spoke with intensity and fervor of a secret message encoded in the blast. If only they knew what it was. The attack incident served as a kind of Rosetta Stone with a secret code waiting to be broken: "We know that God was trying to tell us something," said my UCT student Nadja's mother; "only, the true meaning hasn't yet been revealed." But one older woman, who lost a dear friend in the attack, thought she understood the message: "God has chosen us to give us a sign of His mighty strength. He has told us: Life is given, life is taken away. Live it fully day to day. Be kind to those you love, cherish them now. For you never know if your loved ones will all be wiped out tomorrow. Praise the Lord!" My weak and tentative attempts to introduce the political context and meanings of the massacre were roundly rejected by both the clergy and worshipers. The church was described as apolitical, and their assailants were labeled "criminals," "thugs," and "brutes," delinquents and people without politics. On return visits to the church in 1996 and 1998 during the TRC (Truth and Reconciliation) hearings, the clergy, victims, and survivors of the massacre grew in their understanding of the anger, resentment, and political desperation of the young men who exploded into their quiet, "apolitical," suburban white Capetonian lives. And gradually the young militants convicted of the church attack came to see the worshipers as unfortunate and ill-advised targets of their political struggle. For a great many others the remorse and forgiveness are still forthcoming.

Sacred Wounds

The ability to turn bad into good is a prerequisite of reconciliation, and this ability is aided immeasurably by religious faith. Father Lapsely, an Anglican priest and ANC comrade, who was the target of a letter bomb designed by the South African Security Forces to kill him, maintains that he is a victor and not a victim of apartheid-sponsored political violence. In living each day he defeated evil and death. And like the St. James Church survivors, Fr. Michael believes he was never closer to God than in the transcendent moment of the bomb blast that took away his hands: "I felt whole for the first time when the bomb exploded. I felt the living and true presence of the Holy Spirit who accompanies me and holds me up still." During a visit to Harlem's Canaan Baptist Church Michael told the congregation: "I stand before you as a sign of the power of God to heal, the power of love, of gentleness, of compassion. The power of light is stronger than the power of darkness, and in the power of God we shall be victorious."

The wounded body is a template of individual and collective memory, a map and a moral charter. At the St. James Church Christian coffeehouse, Mrs. K., one of the wounded, pulled back her turtle neck sweater to reveal a large and still inflamed wound on her shoulder where shrapnel was removed and the beginnings of a large, textured scar from neck to shoulder. "Do you know what this means?" she asked. I shook my head. "This wound means I belong to Jesus. He has chosen me. I am His. This wound is precious to me. It has removed all my fears. Nothing can ever hurt me again. Let the 'savages' return. I am ready for them. His mark is upon me. I am His subject. He owns me and my life is in His hands." Her intensity frightened me, and suddenly I wanted to change the subject, even though presumably this is my subject.

The quest to "make sense" of suffering and chaotic violence is as old as Job and as fraught with moral ambiguity for the anthropologist-witness as for Job's companions who demanded an explanation compatible with their own views of a just God. "You must have done something wrong," Job's companions taunted him; but Job steadfastly refused their theodicy. Survivor guilt is real and often takes the form of scapegoating and victim blaming. Here again one thinks of the discussions of ritual scapegoating and sacrifice as discussed by René Girard (1987). Girard built his theory of religion around the idea of sacrificial violence and the need for an agreed-upon surrogate—the "generative scapegoat"—the one, like Jesus, whose suffering or death helps to resolve unbearable social "tensions, conflicts, and material difficulties of all kinds" (1987, 74). The given-up, offered-up comrades in the struggle have been sacrificed in the face of terrible conflicts about collective survival.

Similarly, at the memorial service at the University of the Western Cape the day after Amy Biehl was stoned to death, her angry and grieving friends and colleagues whispered among themselves: "We don't want to blame Amy, of course, but she, of all people, should have known better. What could she have been thinking when she agreed to bring her friends home to Guguletu on that evening?" Guguletu township during those tense days was a veritable No-Go Zone for whites, comrades or not.

Job steadfastly refused the temptation to self-blame, insisting that he had not sinned, that he was a just man. Amy, too, refused the judgment of her attackers, and she approached their raised fists saying, "No, stop. You are mistaken. I am not a settler. I'm Amy, a comrade. I am one of you." Amy's naive claim, coming from her big, white, smiling face, may have further enraged the young men bent on her destruction, but her words returned later to haunt the young men who were ultimately convicted of her death and who later appeared before the Truth and Reconciliation Commission seeking amnesty for a "political" crime. "I feel sorry," Ntbeko Peni ended his testimony before the TRC, "and very down-hearted, especially today when I see that I took part in killing someone we could have used to further our aims. Amy was one of those people who in an international sense could have worked for the country" (1997). And so Ntbeko finally did come to accept that Amy Biehl was, as she said, a comrade.

The danger, as Immanuel Levinas notes, of all theodocies—of all attempts to make coherent and meaningful the suffering of others—is rationalizing and rendering "acceptable" the useless suffering and death of the Other. In all theodocies—anthropological, theological, philosophical, or psychological—the arbitrary character of suffering and death is hidden. The companions of Job return to goad the hurt, the disappeared, the maimed, and the dying: "You must have been into something"; "you must have neglected your religious or your political obligations"; "you yourself must have really wanted to suffer or to die"; "your death is meaningful because it will serve as a lesson to the living." This very flawed but human search for meaning, the attempt to make sense of suffering, has allowed a great many people (Levinas warns) to blame sufferers for their own pain, to value suffering as penance for past sins, as a means to an end, as the price of sensitivity and consciousness, or as the path of saints and martyrs.

If my limited, secular, and anthropological reading of Levinas is correct, the Jewish philosopher is challenging us to consider the opposite: the ultimate meaninglessness and uselessness of the suffering of others. Suffering, Levinas writes, is passivity, pure undergoing, a blow against freedom, an impasse of life and being. It is evil and absurd. Attempts to explain, to account for, another person's pain are the source of all immorality. One may attribute meaning to one's own suffering, but the only ethical way to think about the suffering of the Other is to see it as irremediably tragic and useless, without meaning.

And yet I think of the way that the mothers of the Brazilian shanty-town of Alto do Cruzeiro (Crucifix Hill) consoled each other that their hungry babies died because they were "meant" to die or because they "had" to die. I think of how the Irish mothers of IRA soldiers consoled each other during political wakes and funerals with the belief that their "martyred" children died purposefully and died well and of the similar consolation shared among the South African township mothers. The grieving mother of Amy Biehl, too, whispered to me conspiratorially during a break in the trial of her daughter's alleged killers in Cape Town: "Don't you think there was something destined about Amy's death? Don't you think that for some reason, perhaps not known to us here and now, that Amy had to die?"

Linda Biehl was not the only mother left to ponder the meaning or the necessity of her child's death in the wake of "Operation Barcelona." I think, too, of Mrs. Dolly Mphahlele of Tembisa township, the mother of fifteen-year-old Ernest Mphahlele, who was caught running with a street gang that had been terrorizing the community. When the "young comrades" came looking for Ernest, Dolly knew that her son was as good as dead. But she accepted the harsh "codes" of popular justice that governed township life during the final years of the anti-apartheid struggle and she made only one request to the comrades: "You can kill my son, but do not burn him. The one thing I won't stand for is fire on my son." Her maternal plea was ignored, however, and the next day Mrs. Mphahlele buried the charred remains of Ernest.

Later, during the Biehl trial, I asked Linda to explain further what she had meant in saying that her daughter had to die. In the crypt of St. George's cathedral, over a cup of Roibos tea, Mrs. Biehl leaned over intently: "There is something you need to know about Amy. She was a high achiever, but in the end something always happened to check her, to trip her up. So I wasn't surprised when I heard that she was murdered on the day before she was to leave South Africa. . . . Amy was very competitive, a high diver and a marathon runner. The last photo I have of her is a newspaper clipping of Amy just as she came through the finish line in a marathon. Her face is full of ecstasy, pain, exhaustion, and relief. I like to think that this is what Amy looked like when she died in Guguletu—as if she was just breaking through another, her most difficult finish line."

One can only sympathize with Linda Biehl's desire to substitute an image of beauty and light for the brutal photos attached to Amy's autopsy reports. One can understand her desire to memorialize the stoning of her daughter as a kind of final test, her daughter's last marathon. It must have summoned all of Linda Biehl's faith to allude to Amy as a "martyr" in the tradition of Saint Stephen.

It is a painful sort of accommodationist maternal thinking that would allow a mother—whether Dolly Mphahlele or Linda Biehl—to accept the suffering and death of her own child. But it was redeemed by both women's—among a great many other such examples that have emerged during the course of the TRC hearings—adamantly refusing to condemn their child's killers, who were, in so many like instances, carried away by the excesses of revolutionary violence. Linda Biehl's refusal to condemn her daughter's killers was broadcast and celebrated widely in South Africa, even as it was tearfully and remorsefully accepted by the men and women of St. Gabriel's Church in Guguletu, where Linda and Peter Biehl have become active parishioners in their many and continuous returns to the township. Linda Biehl's faith in the idea of her daughter's meaningful suffering allowed her to approach and embrace the mother of one of her daughter's killers and to publicly forgive the young men and refuse to stand in the way of their applications for political amnesty. Along with a multitude of mothers, sisters, and wives in South Africa who are being called upon to do the same, Linda Biehl summoned her own family's tragedy to serve the larger cause of national healing and reconciliation.

So, even accepting the heightened ethical and theological sensitivity of Immanuel Levinas toward establishing a proper distance and respect toward the suffering of the Other, which should never be turned into an icon of idolatrous faith, who would blame Mrs. Mphahlele, Mrs. Biehl, and the countless victims and survivors of government sponsored violence and the soft targets of retaliatory popular uprisings and terrorist massacres for their search to find some meaning, some transcendent purpose, some beauty even, behind the violence and the suffering? And with that search comes the smallest consolation, which is the first step toward getting over the past and approaching the other side.

Acknowledgment: Field research for this article was supported, in part, by a grant from the Harry Frank Guggenheim Foundation. It was written while the author was a Research Fellow at the Institute on Violence, Culture and Survival at the Virginia Foundation for the Humanities and Public Policy. The article is drawn from the author's forthcoming book, *Who's the Killer? Violence and Democracy in the New South Africa,* to be published by the University of California Press.

Works Cited

Arendt, Hannah. 1963. *Eichmann in Jerusalem: A Report on the Banality of Evil.* New York: Vintage.

———. 1969. *On Violence.* New York: Harcourt, Brace and World.

Basaglia, Franco. 1982. "Le instituzioni di violenza." In *Scritti II, Dall'apertura del manicomio,* ed. Franco Basaglia. Turin: Einaudi.

———. 1986. "Peace-Time Crimes." In *Psychiatry Inside Out: Selected Writings of Franco Basaglia,* ed. Nancy Scheper-Hughes and Anne M. Lovell, 143–226. New York: Columbia University Press.

Benjamin, Walter. 1969. "Theses on the Philosophy of History." In *Illuminations,* ed. Hannah Arendt, 253–64. New York: Schocken.

Bode, Barbara. 1989. *No Bells to Toll: Destruction and Creation in the Andes.* New York: Charles Scribner's Sons.

Bourdieu, Pierre. 1977. *Outline of a Theory of Practice.* Cambridge: Cambridge University Press.

———. 1996. *In Other Words.* Stanford: Stanford University Press.

Daniel, Valentine. 1997. *Charred Lullabies: Chapters in an Anthropology of Violence.* Princeton: Princeton University Press.

Das, Veena. 1997. "Language and the Body: Transactions in the Construction of Pain." *Daedalus* 125 (winter): 67–92.

Fackenheim, Emil. 1970. *God's Presence in History.* New York: New York University Press.

Foucault, Michel. 1979. *Discipline and Punish.* New York: Vintage.

Geertz, Clifford. 1995. *After the Fact.* Cambridge: Harvard University Press.

Geuss, Raymond. 1981. *The Idea of Critical Theory.* Cambridge: Cambridge University Press.

Girard, René. 1987. "Generative Scapegoating." In *Violent Origins: Ritual Killing and Cultural Formation,* ed. Robert G. Hamerton-Kelly, 73–105. Stanford: Stanford University Press.

Goldhagen, Daniel. 1996. *Hitler's Willing Executioners.* New York: Alfred Knopf.

Henry, Jules. 1966. *Sham, Vulnerability, and Other Forms of Self-Destruction.* New York: Vintage.

Kleinman, Arthur, and Joan Kleinman. 1997. "The Appeal of Experience; The Dismay of Images: Cultural Appropriations of Suffering in our Times." In *Social Suffering,* ed. A. Kleinman, V. Das, and M. Lock, 1–23. Berkeley: University of California Press.

Kleinman, A., V. Das, and M. Lock, eds. *Social Suffering.* Berkeley: University of California Press.

Levinas, Immanuel. 1986. "Useless Suffering." In *Face to Face with Levinas,* ed. Richard A. Cohen, 156–67. New York: State University of New York Press.

Lévi-Strauss, Claude. 1995. *Saudades do Brasil.* Seattle: University of Washington Press.

Malkki, Lisa. 1996. *Purity in Exile.* Chicago: University of Chicago Press.

Olujic, Maria. 1998. "Children and War in the Former Yugoslavia." In *Small Wars: The Cultural Politics of Childhood*, ed. N. Scheper-Hughes and C. Sarcent, 318–30. Berkeley: University of California Press.

Peni, Ntbeko. 1997. *Daily Mail and Guardian*, 8 July.

Sacks, Oliver. 1985. *The Man Who Mistook His Wife for a Hat*. New York: Simon and Schuster.

Scheper-Hughes, Nancy. 1979. *Saints, Scholars and Schizophrenics: Mental Illness in Rural Ireland*. Berkeley: University of California Press.

———. 1992. *Death without Weeping: The Violence of Everyday Life in Brazil*. Berkeley: University of California Press.

———. 1996. "Small Wars and Invisible Genocides." *Social Science & Medicine* 43, no. 5:889–900.

———. 1997. "Peace Time Crimes." *Social Identities* 3, no. 3:471–97.

———. 1998. "The New Cannibalism: The Global Trade in Human Organs." *New Internationalist* 300 (April): 14–17.

Starn, Orin. 1992. "Missing the Revolution: Anthropologists and the War in Peru." In *Rereading Cultural Anthropology*, ed. George Marcus, 152–80. Durham: Duke University Press.

Taussig, Michael. 1989. *The Nervous System*. New York: Routledge.

Weschler, Lawrence. 1990. *A Miracle, a Universe: Settling Accounts with Torturers*. New York: Viking.

Staging Violence against Women

A Long Series of Replays

Lesley Ferris

Prologue

AS THEATRE EDUCATORS we often find ourselves sitting through performances against our will. Recently I attended a performance of *Kiss Me Kate* produced by a long-active community theatre. I had convinced myself that it was worth going to hear even an amateur rendering of "Brush Up Your Shakespeare," and I was accompanied by my thirteen-year-old daughter, who was nurturing a newly discovered passion for singing.

Kate's first encounter with Petruchio takes place in front of the entire chorus. He swaggers on stage, full of machismo, prominently displaying a large whip. At this, my daughter whispered to me, "Are they all just going to stand there and watch? And do nothing?" And later, when a groveling Kate crawled on the floor, my daughter whispered again, "They've just made her stupid."

Another evening of theatrical spectating brought me to a small professional production of *The Fantasticks,* this time accompanied by both of my daughters. As the play progressed, I sat in utter amazement as the two older male characters, the fathers of the two young lovers, sang a song entitled "Rape." The forced comic tone of their rendition failed to elicit any laughter from the audience. Obviously, I was not the only one who wondered why this song—clearly outmoded—had been kept. At the intermission my daughters told me that they thought the song was "disgusting," and I asked the management why it had been left in the show despite the fact that so many people found it offensive. I was told that the authors of the piece had created a new song to replace it because it was clearly inappropriate for a 1990s audience but that the director of the musical, for some unexplained reason, chose to keep the original.

At roughly the same time that I viewed these performances, I was invited to take part in *Theatre Symposium*'s "Theatre and Violence" conference. Thus my experience of watching *Kiss Me Kate* and *The Fantasticks* immediately foregrounded what is for me the continuing conundrum of theatrical violence and its relation to women.

In particular, I was struck by the paradoxical nature of theatre—that it is ephemeral and fleeting and at the same time immersed in repetition. In the commercial world a play needs to be repeated enough times to make money. The theatrical canon comprises plays that have been produced throughout decades and centuries. And, finally, theatre is an art form in which, through repetition, the body learns and memorizes gestures, language, and perhaps even emotions, thus ensuring that the live performance can be replayed in the future (remember that the French word for rehearsal is *répétition*). The following essay explores instances of theatrical violence against women in the context of this notion of repetition.

Violence and Spectacle

Actual violence against women and the public display of such violence in TV, film, and other media create such a relentless background to our daily lives that many questions and concerns arise when a director selects a play that foregrounds such violence. Does such staged violence comment on and criticize the dramatic events? Or does it merely reinforce the status quo, a position that often seems to celebrate the actress as a theatrical spectacle of victimhood? Hélène Cixous, in her theatre essay, "Aller à la Mer," questions "how, as women, can we go to the theatre without lending our complicity to the sadism directed against women, or being asked to assume, in the patriarchal family structure that the theatre reproduces ad infinitum, the position of the victim?" (546). As women, how do we portray these roles, direct these plays, stage such violence? How do we extricate ourselves from the role of the victim that pervades and even dominates so many theatre texts?

In conceiving this article I have identified two specific areas of the larger issue of women and dramatic violence: women who are paragons of virtue and have some form of violence done to them unjustly (e.g., Desdemona, Hermione, the thousand heroines of nineteenth-century melodrama); and women who are either seen as violent or "unnaturally" aggressive themselves (Miss Julie, Clytemnestra) or are simply strong and wilful (the Duchess of Malfi). In my study I will examine briefly some key canonical texts by males that focus on these topics.

In Shakespeare's *Much Ado About Nothing, Othello,* and *A Winter's Tale,* a group of plays that are linked thematically, a central female character is accused of adultery by her husband or betrothed. In each case the woman is never consulted, and her guilt is assumed and upheld. Also, in each the woman is removed from the scene through "death." Hero, in *Much Ado About Nothing,* pretends to die in order to remove herself from the painful accusations of the man she loves; Desdemona is murdered by Othello; and Hermione disappears for sixteen years and is believed by her accusing husband to be dead. Thus, in the worlds of these plays, simply to think a woman unfaithful consigns her to punishment.

Because in each case the accused woman is utterly innocent of the charges, Shirley Nelson Garner sees the acts of violence against these women as a reassertion of male power. She argues:

> [T]hat Shakespeare wanted to depict his male characters as needing to be betrayed is further affirmed by their determination to believe that they are betrayed. When a moment . . . comes that the contrary might be true, that the women they suspect might be faithful, they insist on their falseness. . . . The male characters' certainty of betrayal allows them to unleash their pent-up misogyny and fear of women as they plot vengeance, revile their beloveds and women in general and persecute and even murder or attempt to murder the innocent women who love them. Their distrust also allows them to break their bonds with those women and return either imaginatively or actually to an exclusive male community. (Garner 1983)

Garner's notion of an "exclusive male community" rings even more true, perhaps, when we reflect on the practices of the Elizabethan stage itself—a public space that permitted only males to have access to the art of theatre. Can we consider this, à la Cixous, a double act of violence? Are these women who are rendered unto death within the theatrical narrative also excluded (virtually dead) from the practice of the art?

Cixous further claims that theatre is more violent than fiction because of its ability to repeat and intensify "the horror of the murder scene"—a scene in which women are essential for the purpose of eliminating them: "[O]nly when [the woman] has disappeared can the curtain go up; she is relegated to repression, to the grave, the asylum, oblivion and silence. When she does make an appearance she is doomed, ostracized or in a waiting-room. She is loved only when absent or abused, a phantom or a fascinating abyss" (546).

I now turn to my second category: wilful women. To do so I return to the "notorious" Kate (a role that is arguably the most difficult in Shakespeare's canon for a contemporary actress to play) and to the tradition of shrew tales that underlie Shakespeare's text. Here history is instructive. Historians and scholars generally agree that between 1560 and 1642 in Britain there was a "crisis of order." This sense of crisis often involved female rebellion and intimations of female independence. Indeed, fears relating to the possibility of such insubordination led John Knox to articulate his concerns about the troubling number of female rulers throughout Europe in a famous misogynistic treatise, *The First Blast of the Trumpet Against the Monstrous Regiment of Women.*

Literary attacks upon and defenses of women were widespread in European literature of the late Middle Ages and the Renaissance. These attacks and defenses were so much in evidence that discussions on the "Nature of Woman" were recognized as a formal controversy. Shrew-taming tales were a staple of this literature, from poetry, to prose anecdote, to scenes in drama, to entire plays. In 1557 Erasmus's influential work on marriage was translated into English as *A merry dialogue, declaring the properties of shrewed shrews, and honest wives.* The wifely policy Erasmus recommended, and which found numerous imitators and adapters, was submissiveness. The popularity of some of these works was staggering. Between 1616 and 1634, for example, Joseph Swetnam's misogynistic pamphlet, *Arraignment of lewd, idle, froward and inconstant women,* which was preoccupied with rebellious, wilful women, went through ten editions.

Possibly one of the most brutal of the extant shrew-taming stories is the anonymous *A Merry Jest of a Shrewde and curst Wife lapped in Morrelles skin,* which appeared in the early English Renaissance. In this tale the shrew is tamed on her wedding night when the new husband keeps her awake all night, hits her, rips up her clothes, and forces her to adopt various positions. Finally, the groom "drags her into a deep cellar . . . beats her bloody from head to toe with birch rods, and wraps her senseless body in the salted hide of Morel, a horse he has had killed for the purpose. When the salt in her wounds revives her and her husband threatens to keep her in Morel's skin for the rest of her life, the wife vows eternal submission" (Woodbridge 202).

Another significant aspect of this version of the shrew story and common to many others is the author's insistence on having witnesses available to view the wife's various humiliations. The bride's mother visits the couple during their wedding night to check on the progress of consummation, and later the bride's family and friends visit for dinner to witness the wife's submission. Even the birch rods and the horse's skin, proudly displayed as signs of the husband's triumphant success and the wife's humiliating defeat, become objects of the family's vo-yeuristic pleasure.

The importance of visual spectacle in relation to these often grisly tales resonated in the Renaissance community rituals for dealing with shrewish women. It was common practice in local villages for domineering women or unruly wives to be publicly shamed. For these spectacles of shaming to be most effective, it was important that the punished women were viewed by as many people as possible. In one form of punishment, the accused woman was put in a scold's collar or ridden about in a cart by a procession of villagers to the accompaniment of rough music (banging pots and pans). Another form utilized the dunking stool, a punishment in which a woman was strapped to a stool, lowered into a small pond, and held under water for brief periods of time.

By the time Shakespeare wrote *The Taming of the Shrew,* he was part of a long literary tradition of shrew-taming tales. You could say he knew a good money-making plot when he saw one. Because knowledge of the basic plot was commonplace, the play's popularity was assured. Although by the time he was writing for his company, the physical brutality of the shrew-taming jests had diminished considerably, the scopic element of humiliation and psychological torment remained ever present.

It is also significant that the popularity of shrew-taming tales paralleled the height of accusations against women concerning witchcraft. Close examination of the text of *Taming of the Shrew* shows that Kate's father, Baptista, links her with the devil through his line, "thou hilding of a devilish spirit" (2.1.26); Hortensio threatens Kate with a ride in a "cart" (a form of punishment for overbearing or talkative wives); and one of Petruchio's techniques of abuse in taming Kate is to prevent her from sleeping, a practice commonly used by the witchfinders of Britain to obtain the necessary confession from the accused woman.

A further problem in dealing with this particular script is the way in which Kate's language is at odds with her eponymous role as the shrew. Fiona Shaw, the British actress who tackled the role of Kate in a 1987 production directed by Jonathan Miller, found this particular element difficult: "[T]here's a breakdown of language at the beginning of the play. Petruchio has all the lines. This woman, who is so eloquent at the end of the play, has no language at the beginning, she doesn't even speak great truths about the community" (Shaw 138).

The acknowledged difficulty of dramatizing in *The Taming of the Shrew* what is essentially a form of wife beating on the stage continues to attract directors who wish to solve this dilemma. Michael Bogdanov, in a recent production by the Royal Shakespeare Company, had Kate deliver her infamous final speech of wifely submission with "smoldering resentment and hostility, while the men, uncomprehending, lie back and listen with smug satisfaction" (Epstein 87). In the 1990 New York Shakespeare Festival production, which was set in the wild west and featured Tracey Ullman and Morgan Freeman, Ullman ended the speech by accidentally whopping Petruchio and sending him sprawling (Headrick). Charles Marowitz's adaptation, entitled *The Shrew*, compared Petruchio's taming tactics to the brainwashing techniques used on prisoners of war. Kate's final speech was delivered in a dull, robotic, monotonous tone, as if she had learned it by rote (Epstein 88).

Yet another difficulty in staging Shakespeare's *The Taming of the Shrew* and in interpreting the role of Kate is that the play (which is always listed under the heading of "Romantic Comedy," along with *Twelfth Night, As You Like It,* and *Love's Labours Lost*) is an example of the ways in which issues of violence have historically become intertwined with comedy. Likewise, the anonymous author of the *Wife lapped in Morrelles skin* referred to his tale as a "merry jest," and shrew-taming tales were regularly found in Renaissance jest books. As Linda Woodbridge points out in her important work *Women and the English Renaissance,* authors of these stories "seem to have assumed that the physical torment and psychological humiliation of a woman would strike readers as side-splittingly funny, filling them with mirth and good spirits" (204).

I have argued in my book, *Acting Women,* that the 'wilful woman' is a central female image in our theatrical canon—an image riven by its own double-edged meaning of adult strength and childish obstinacy. Although shrew-taming tales are consigned to the realm of comedy and the Kates of this world are consigned to conjugal submission, the majority of wilful women in the dramatic canon are tragic figures who must be murdered, eradicated from the script, consigned, as Cixous states, into the abyss, the absence (546). These figures include Clytemnestra and the Duchess of Malfi. Their transgressions are essentially sexual; they have acted autonomously and chosen their own sexual partners. As Virginia Woolf stated in *A Room of One's Own,* "[T]he daughter who refused to marry the gentleman of her parents' choice was liable to be locked up, beaten and flung about the room, without any shock being inflicted on public opinion. Marriage was not an affair of personal affection, but of family avarice, particularly in the 'chivalrous' upper classes" (41–42).

Several centuries earlier Matteo Bandello, the Renaissance writer who first wrote down the story of the Duchess of Malfi, explained: "Would that we were not daily forced to hear that one man has murdered his wife because he suspected her of infidelity; that another has killed his daughter on account of a secret marriage; that a third has caused his sister to be murdered because she would not marry as he wished! It is a great cruelty that we claim the right to do whatever we list and will not suffer women to do the same. If they do anything which does not please us there we are at once with cords and daggers and poison" (cited by Hawkins 340).

For Bandello, and for Webster who followed him, the story of the Duchess is told to enlist us on the side of the victim, to confront horrors so extreme and social injustices so utterly senseless and cruel that we cannot but join in and react against them. Yet the story of the murder of the Duchess, her children, and her husband is told within the social context of less extreme measures. Women who did not obey, for example, could be "locked up, beaten and flung about the room, without any shock being inflicted on public opinion." The implication here is frightening: Although murder may be going too far, a mere beating is socially acceptable.

From the theatre's inception violence has remained at the very core of the dramatic impulse, so it is hardly surprising that some of the earliest plays in the Western canon focus on women who transgress. *The Oresteia*, the trilogy by Aeschylus, receives its dramatic impetus from a series of murders, and the final matricide of Clytemnestra both ends the cycle of violence and initiates the patriarchy. Like the Duchess of Malfi, Clytemnestra has chosen her own sexual partner, and like the Duchess she is murdered; but unlike the Duchess, she has murdered and thus for the Greeks has come to represent the archetypal wilful, unruly, monstrous woman—a kind of woman embodied on the stage by the presence of her terrifying, writhing Furies.

Clytemnestra, like Eve in another founding myth of the patriarchy, has been stripped of any sense of individuality and thereby has come to signify the transgressions of all women. Homer described her in *The Odyssey*: "[B]y her utter wickedness of will she has poured dishonor both on herself and every woman that lives hereafter, even on one [whose] deeds are virtuous" (XI, 433–35). In these two literary myths of female punishment, wherein one female act of hubris brings a curse on the entire House of Women, there is a discernible pattern: All women must suffer because of Eve, just as all women must accept male dominance and submission because of Clytemnestra.

The Greeks were particularly fascinated by homicidal females and represented them in visual, as well as literary, narratives. Numerous vase paintings portray Clytemnestra with ax in hand running toward an open door, a reinforcement of the Aeschylean view of her as the evil, anarchic, unruly female (Keuls 338). Aeschylus pursues this threat of strong, husband-killing women even further in his play *The Suppliants*. Here the Danaids (fifty daughters of Daneus) rebel against proposed marriages to their male cousins. These militant virgins are forced to undergo the marriage ceremony, but on their wedding night they murder their bridegrooms. A second mass marital murder takes place in a lost play by Sophocles that featured a group of Lemnian women who massacred their mates and established a "manless" society. Froma Zeitlin views these male-generated visions of masculine slaughter as an "Amazon" complex that "envisions that woman's refusal of her required subordinate role must, by an inevitable sequence, lead to its opposite: total domination, gynecocracy, whose extreme form projects the enslavement or murder of men. The same polarizing imagination can only conceive of two hierarchic alternatives: Rule by Men and Rule by Women" (153).

In all of these stories of women who murder their men, one female character invariably refuses the anarchic actions of her sisters, choosing instead a submissive loyalty to the male line. In the Lemnian massacre a good daughter spares her father out of filial piety, and in the myth of the Danaids a single woman refrains from murdering her new husband. Even in the singular story of Clytemnestra, the Furies (the personification of her corrupted, depraved femininity) undergo a startling metamorphosis when Athena transforms them into the Eumenides, gentle, pacified priestesses who agree to promote marriage and fertility for the good of the state.[1]

In all of these violent acts the murders occur in the privacy of the home, even in the bedchamber. The one exception to this scenario is the story of the Amazons who confront male authority publicly on the battlefield. The legendary Amazons were extremely popular as quintessential rebellious, unconventional, disorderly women, and the Amazonmachia (the battle between the Greeks and the Amazons) became a central symbol in Greek culture of the victory of the male over the female. As Keuls explains, the Amazon motif is one of the most characteristic themes in Athenian mythology (along with the motif of rape). She describes it as one of the "charter myths" of Athenian society and as one of the most ubiquitous images on Attic monuments: "[W]herever an Athenian turned his eyes, he was likely to encounter the effigy of one of his mythological ancestors, stabbing or clubbing an Amazon to death" (34).

---

[1]The Amazonian legend carries its own submissive female as well. In the Homeric episode of the Amazons one of the female leaders, Antiope, is captured by Theseus and alters her warrior persona to become a faithful wife and mother.

One of the first literary renderings of the Amazon myth, a view of the wilful, unruly woman that perhaps stretches across centuries and connects to our own concerns about violence in society in general and violence against women in particular, is found in a lost epic poem entitled *Aithiopis*. In this early version, perhaps recorded in the seventh century B.C., the Greeks defeated a group of exotic women warriors who came to defend the besieged city of Troy. Athenian mythology added a new dimension, as Amazons invaded the Greek homeland and were defeated by the popular hero Theseus. Keuls states that "this addition had the double effect of tying early Attic history in with the glorious epic past of the Greeks, and of creating a mythological male-female confrontation connected with the origins of Athenian society" (45).

Although the staging of murders was forbidden on the Greek stage and the dramatic violence took place offstage, there seems to have been no concern about the representation of violence and murder in other art forms such as vase painting, sculpture, and painting. So central was the Amazonmachia to the Greek image of itself that it was depicted on the shield of Athena Parthenos and on the western metopes of the Parthenon, the center of Greek democratic pride and power. For Athenian citizens the story of their victory over the insubordinate Amazons was both myth and historical reality. The murder of these rebellious women was regularly included, as was the downfall of the Persians, in the numerous eulogies and funeral orations that celebrated their glorious deeds and promoted Athenian patriotism.

Within the numerous images of Greeks stabbing, goring, piercing, or clubbing Amazons, one additional representation deserves special mention: the slaying of the Amazon queen, Penthesileia, by the Greek Achilles. This particular encounter is perhaps the most poignant and also the most troubling. According to the myth, Achilles killed Penthesileia, but at the very moment he pierced her breast, he fell in love with her. A drinking cup from the classical period, considered one of the most outstanding surviving artifacts from the era, depicts the moment of death entwined with the moment of acknowledged passion: "The Amazon has fallen on her knees before Achilles and is caressing his breast in a gesture of seduction. Achilles' sword is piercing her from above; in other words, the hero has stabbed her while she was pleading for mercy, but the magic moment has arrived: there is eye contact between the two and the ardent expression on Achilles' face indicates that he is responding to the pleading, but too late" (Keuls 47).

Could this image be read as a move toward understanding, toward conciliation? Or is it more likely that the penile sword presents a troubling image of sexual desire combined with murderous violence? If the latter is true, then it is sobering to locate within the cultural origins of Western art a precursor of the snuff movie. And if theatre is an art of repetition and memory, are we doomed to keep playing these images, these songs, these dramatic moments over and over again?

Works Cited

Cixous, Hélène. 1984. "Aller à la Mer." Trans. Barbara Kerslake. *Modern Drama* 24, no. 4:546–52.

Epstein, Norrie. 1993. *The Friendly Shakespeare*. New York: Penguin Books.

Ferris, Lesley. 1990. *Acting Women: Images of Women in Theatre*. London: Macmillan.

Garner, Shirley Nelson. 1983. "Male Bonding and the Myth of Women's Deception in Shakespeare's Plays." Paper delivered at the American Theatre Association Annual Conference. Minneapolis, Minn.

Hawkins, Harriet. 1975. "The Victim's Side: Chaucer's *Clerk's Tale* and Webster's *Duchess of Malfi*." *Signs: Journal of Women in Culture and Society* 1:339–61.

Headrick, Charlotte J. 1991. " 'Our Lances Are but Straws': Solving the Problem of Kate's Last Speech in *The Taming of the Shrew*." Paper delivered at NEH Seminar/East Tennessee Shakespeare in the Park.

Keuls, Eva C. 1985. *The Reign of the Phallus: Sexual Politics in Ancient Athens*. Berkeley: University of California Press.

Shakespeare, William. 1959. *The Complete Works of Shakespeare*. London: Oxford University Press.

Shaw, Fiona. 1991. "Fiona Shaw: Like Walking on Blades Every Night." In *'Sheer Bloody Magic': Conversations with Actresses,* ed. Carole Woddis. London: Virago Press.

Woodbridge, Linda. 1984. *Women and the English Renaissance: Literature and the Nature of Womankind*. Urbana: University of Illinois Press.

Woolf, Virginia. 1977. *A Room of One's Own*. London: Grafton Books.

Zeitlin, Froma I. 1987. "The Dynamics of Misogyny: Myth and Mythmaking in the *Oresteia*." *Aresthusa* 2:149–184.

The Scenic Ideals of Roman Blood Spectacles and Their Role in the Development of Amphitheatrical Space

James Harley

THE DECLINE IN THE PERFORMANCE of new, regular drama in Rome in the first century B.C. and the concurrent rise in the popularity of public blood spectacles have generally been attributed by later scholars to a larger process of moral degeneration among the Roman populace and to certain of its more notorious emperors.[1] Although such narratives may be convenient as frameworks through which to consider or perhaps teach complex periods of historical transition, closer study of such periods inevitably reveals the gaps and rough edges that have been glossed over in the narrative's construction. For modern theatre scholars dealing with ancient Rome, separating narrative from fact is especially problematic, primarily because we come into the area so long after these overarching moral/historical narratives have been established and accepted as valid interpretive lenses. Indeed, past scholars in our field, with predetermined conclusions dictated by the narrative (and sympathetic to the same moral logic that produced it), have "deduced" the odious nature of Roman blood spectacles and, rather than engaging the theatrically significant question of the dynamics of their aesthetic appeal to audiences, have sought mainly to rationalize their onerous existence.[2]

---

[1] I use the terms *bloodsports* and *blood spectacles* to refer to staged animal hunts (venationes), gladiatorial contests, and public executions.

[2] For examples see Beare 21; Grant; and Isaac.

However, in foregrounding the moral aspect of the blood spectacles as the key to their eventual triumph over regular drama, historians have marginalized the substantial aesthetic alterations that also accompanied their success. Indeed, it is demonstrable that the Imperial blood spectacles incorporated aesthetic conventions borrowed directly from theatrical performance in order to enhance their popular appeal, including (but not limited to) the use of costuming, music, and even plots based on existing dramas (Coleman 44–73). In fact, the popularity of the blood spectacles did not surpass that of the theatre until the reign of Augustus (27 B.C.–A.D. 14), when a number of measures were consciously employed to increase the scenic appeal of these morbid events. This process of aesthetic elaboration reached its peak nearly a century later in the highly theatrical public executions sponsored by Nero, who reigned from A.D. 54 to 68, and in the inauguration of the Roman Colosseum as the ideal site for blood spectacles in A.D. 80.

It is my purpose to examine briefly the spatial and scenic elaboration of the blood spectacles in order to suggest that each phase in the development of the amphitheatre brought a better facility, not only for viewing the increasing (and perhaps morally degenerate) judicial violence of Imperial Rome but equally for appealing to the traditional aesthetic sensibilities of the populace by providing the scenic means to couch that violence within the framework of a performative spectacle. By de-emphasizing the moral character of these events and focusing rather on their aesthetic orchestration, I hope to draw conclusions of greater concrete value for performance scholars. Central to this argument is the scenic relationship of amphitheatrical spaces to conventional theatre spaces in Rome, for indeed, although existing theatres were adequate for viewing and carrying out the violence itself, the aesthetic and scenic ideals of the blood spectacles as a performance event dictated the development of this new type of space.

Accounts by Livy and Valerius Maximus indicate that the first gladiatorial displays in Rome (in 264 B.C.) took place in the Forum Boarium, the public cattle market, a venue whose scenic capabilities and spectatorial capacity were somewhat limited, although it did possess holding space for animals and gladiators, which was essential to the design of the events (Livy 553; Valerius Maximus 123). Stimulated by the tradition of festal competition in Rome, which encouraged sponsors to constantly surpass one another in the scale of their spectacles, the number of gladiators participating in these exhibitions soon increased (from 6 to more than 250), as did the frequency of the events themselves. The larger, and thereby more spectacular, displays attracted larger audiences, until it became customary to hold these events in the forum Romanum, which, according to Vitruvius, was modified with temporary seating for these occasions (Vitruvius 5.1; Auguet 26).

Meanwhile, the wild animal hunts, not yet linked to gladiatorial exhibitions, were held in the Circus. There, because there were no traps nor hypogeia (substructural passages), animals were sometimes concealed until their entrance inside cages masked as scenic structures (a wooden ship, in one instance) that were usually adjoined to the central spine (euripus metae) of the track (Coleman 52). The fact that such efforts were made to facilitate spectacular central entrances, when numerous passages and portals existed around the side of the track, indicates the *performative* and *scenic* character of these slaughters. Finally, at the same time, the third type of blood spectacle, public executions, occurred in various places about town, with crucifixions often occurring at prominent crossroads.

Despite Vitruvius's advice to construct fora with the requirements of spectacles in mind, Augustus's combination of these three discrete entertainments, each with its own particular demands, into a single spectacle necessitated the rapid assimilation of a more flexible type of space—the amphitheatre—a design probably borrowed from the Campanians. Its 360° elliptical auditorium offering twice the seating capacity of traditional theatres, this new space was also required in Rome because the Forum and circuses could not be retrofitted with sufficient machinery and hypogeia to handle the combined spectacle and still maintain their primary and permanent functions (Vitruvius 5.2; Saunders 93). In fact, before Augustus merged these events even the few model amphitheatres were not fully equipped for the Roman scenic ideal, again indicating the important role of blood spectacles in the ultimate development of this space. For example, the early provincial amphitheatre at Pompeii constructed in 75 B.C. had no traps nor substructures for the handling of scenery and animals and had only two entrances to the playing space (Balsdon 306). Thus it was more limited, scenically, than the Roman forum, which had at least been retrofitted with some substructural passages. But in the first amphitheatre at Rome built by Curio a mere fifteen years later, the shifting scenic ideal is clearly evident. A record of this unusual space, supplied by the elder Pliny, describes it as having been composed of two distinct hemicyclical theatres set back-to-back on individual pivots. The two separate spaces were said to have formed a single amphitheatre when rotated 180 degrees on their pivots. An increasingly accepted view of this description, however, is that it is not a literal representation of Curio's theatre but an attempt by Pliny to describe the nature of amphitheatrical space in general and to account for the term *amphitheatre* itself (Grant 80). If this is so, and

Pliny conceived of the amphitheatre in this way (that is, as a double theatre), it might indicate a prevalent attitude toward the perception of its heightened scenic possibilities.

But what were the scenic possibilities of the amphitheatre, and how did they compare to those of conventional theatre spaces? To begin with, the performance space in the average amphitheatre was substantially larger than in even the largest theatres. The monumental theatre of Pompey, for example, built in 55 B.C., may have contained as much as six hundred square meters of playing space (including orchestra) that was fixed in a single, standard Greek-influenced configuration. By contrast, a typical amphitheatre with an elliptical playing space of only 50 × 30 meters offered about twice the space. The largest amphitheatre, the Roman Colosseum, finished around A.D. 80, had an arena fully 88 × 54 meters. Although a larger space in itself does not necessarily dictate greater spectacle, the increasing size of the venues for bloodsports— moving from the market square, to the forum, and passing over the already existing theatres of Rome to settle in the amphitheatres—indicates a perception of the spatial inadequacy of conventional theatrical sites for the type of spectacle being offered. Although one may reductively attribute this progression to the demands of increasing popularity or population (that is, to the need for greater seating capacity), this notion overlooks the fact that in all of these shifts greater scenic possibilities were also realized. This added potential is a function not only of the increasing size of the space but also of the alteration of its very nature and of the new substructural designs clearly efficacious to scenic enhancement. Thus, the changing aesthetic toward a larger spectacle was reflected concretely in the change of venue.

Accompanying the larger playing space of the amphitheatre was a restructured relationship between performance space and auditorium. The most notable characteristic was the heightened centrality of the amphitheatre's performance space, which was fully surrounded by spectators. Roland Auguet suggests that this factor was prominent in the conception of amphitheatrical space in Rome and links it to other efforts of scenic elaboration: "[M]uch attention had indeed been paid to astounding the public by novelties and eccentricities of staging, but, in the middle of the first century BC, no one had yet considered improving the comfort of the spectators" (26). These new elliptical spaces greatly expanded the seating capacity close to the playing space, thus affording that comfort, as well as clearly focusing attention into the large arena itself. It has also been argued that the choice of elliptical over circular playing space was "optimum" in terms of the scenic ideals of staged

battles in that it provided a longer area over which to advance and re-
treat (Wiedemann 20).

Perhaps what most clearly demonstrates the influence of the desire
for heightened spectacle in the evolution of the arena is the extent to
which these spaces were technically equipped for scenic effects. As noted
above, the amphitheatre at Pompeii had no substructure and thus was
probably not originally intended for animal hunts or spectacular executions involving large numbers of people. The immense Circus, although
sufficient and perhaps even scenically conducive to animal hunts because
of the cover afforded by its central spine, likewise had little supporting
space for storage and holding, and its long, narrow shape was not conducive to viewing gladiatorial combats (Humphrey 186).

The theatre of Pompey in Rome might seem a likely space to which
the unified bloodsports might have been transferred because it was the
largest theatre space available and could provide both adequate scenic
support and viewing capacity if bloodletting were the simple appeal of
the shows. The fact that it was not used for such displays, however,
suggests, again, that although it was scenically sufficient for dramatic
presentations, it was seen as inadequate to meet the *scenic* demands of
bloodsports.

This interpretation is supported by the conditions under which
Pompey's theatre was constructed. Before 55 B.C. the Roman senate
steadfastly resisted the construction of permanent theatres within
Rome, basing their objections on the association of theatre with idleness
and immorality. Pompey, however, found a loophole in this restriction
and, as Tertullian notes, built his theatre as a temple to the Goddess
Venus Victrix, "under which [he] placed steps for viewing shows" (Tertullian 10.5). Because this space was defined and justified as a temple, it
can reasonably be assumed that its scenic devices were limited or at least
not prominent. Indeed, examination of the plans for the theatre show
it to have been highly monumental and ornate but to have offered no
substantially greater staging possibilities than the Hellenistic theatres
that preceded it or the Roman ones that followed (Hanson 120).

The scenic shortcomings of all of these spaces for housing blood spectacles clearly informed the design of later amphitheatres. Although the
primary practical requirement for public bloodlettings was a large
amount of space to house the animals, condemned criminals, and gladiators either beneath the floor of the arena or in the immediate vicinity,
the scenic ideals of the event as performance dictated flexible accessibil-
ity to the arena floor so that scenic effects, such as those used in the
staged executions of criminals "characterized" as mythic figures, might

be orchestrated. In one notable case, an "Orpheus" occupied a central position in the arena as first foliage and then trained animals, seemingly enchanted by the music of the accompanying lyre, apparently rose from the traps and moved toward him as in the mythic tale. Following this scenic and dramatic building of suspense came the ironic twist in the staging as "the earth yawned suddenly and sent forth a she-bear," which mangled the condemned prisoner-made-actor (Coleman 63).

The Flavian Amphitheatre (Roman Colosseum) provides perhaps the best example of the cultivation of such scenic capabilities. In addition to its mile of subterranean passages, the Colosseum was equipped with an elaborate system of holding cells, as well as a number of elevators that were used to transport animals, humans, and scenery up to the arena itself. These elements might pass through plentiful trapdoors in the arena floor or be placed at or released from numerous side entrances. That the trapping potential was noteworthy is clear in Apuleius's report that forests "grew" from the arena floor in clear sight of the spectators and that whole wooden mountains, complete with running streams and live goats not only rose but then descended during one venatio (Apuleius 10.30–10.34). Although such spectacular accounts may exaggerate the effectiveness of the illusion, it is nonetheless clear that scenic effects were central to the appeal of the bloodletting.

Of course, the scale of the spectacles became so great, incorporating thousands of human and animal participants, that ultimately the amphitheatre's substructure itself was inadequate to house the performers, scenery, and machinery required. At this point a separate building, known as the *summum choragium* and accessible to the arena via underground passages, was constructed adjacent to the Colosseum during the reign of Domitian. Ludwig Friedlander characterizes this as essentially a "prop room" for Imperial spectacles, again stressing the importance of scenic support in the presentation of violence in the arena (Friedlander 72).

That aesthetic considerations dictated the development of alternative spaces is also evident in the rarity of the Roman practice of adapting existing Greek and Hellenistic theatres in the provinces for bloodsports. Because this adaptation was, in fact, practiced, these modified theatres must have been capable of containing the bloodsports, but the proliferation of actual amphitheatres outside Rome in the early empire (about 250 have been identified) attests to the desire for a better or more sufficient type of space for the new popular entertainment. Indeed, in the eastern empire, it became conventional to "overlay or supersede" existing theatres with new amphitheatres, as at Dodona in Epirus and Xanthus in Asia Minor (Grant 87). Thus, it appears that the aesthetic considerations of the bloodsports (and not simply the goal of efficacious bloodletting) played a substantial role in the development of the amphitheatre.

It is particularly difficult to discern exactly what motivated the Romans in their far-flung endeavors because by the time of the empire they were an extremely diverse culture, a fact well noted in historical literature. Yet many scholars, indebted to early Christian assessments of the empire, still insist on defining them monolithically via the rubric of "morality" rather than negotiating their boundaries as a complex and fragmented civilization. By suggesting the inadequacy of existing theatres to serve the particularly large scenic demands of bloodsports, and by demonstrating that the amphitheatres were designed with scenic support for the bloodletting in mind, and not simply as sites for efficient and observed killing, I have shown that there was a significant formal component in the Roman taste for bloody entertainment. This formal aspect was, of course, most clearly evident in the actual staging of the blood spectacles, as the brief example of "Orpheus" forcefully illustrates.[3] Furthermore, rather than corroborating the moral-historical narrative of the continuous decline of Republican virtue as the defining aspect of the Empire, the formal (i.e., scenic and dramatic) elaboration of the blood spectacles, borrowing and adapting the conventions and spaces of other popular forms, can as easily be contextualized as a product of a consistent Roman aesthetic fascination with spectacle, novelty, and variety that transcended Rome's political-historical divisions.

Works Cited

Apuleius. 1994. *The Golden Ass*. Trans. P. G. Walsh. Oxford: Clarendon Press.

Auguet, Roland. 1972. *Cruelty and Civilization: The Roman Games*. London: George Unwin.

Balsdon, J. P. V. D. 1969. *Life and Leisure in Ancient Rome*. New York: McGraw-Hill.

Beare, W. 1964. *The Roman Stage: A Short History of Latin Drama in the Time of the Republic*. 3d ed. London: Methuen.

Coleman, K. M. 1990. "Fatal Charades: Roman Executions Staged as Mythological Enactments." *Journal of Roman Studies* 80:44–73.

Friedlander, Ludwig. 1965. *Roman Life and Manners under the Early Empire*. 7th ed. Vol. II. New York: Barnes & Noble.

---

[3]The staging of blood spectacles as performance is treated at greater length in James Harley, "The Aesthetics of Death: The Theatrical Elaboration of Ancient Roman Blood Spectacles." *Theatre History Studies* 18 (1998): 89–97.

Grant, Michael. 1968. *Gladiators.* New York: Delacorte Press.

Hanson, John Arthur. 1959. *Roman Theatre-Temples.* Princeton: Princeton University Press.

Harley, James. 1998. "The Aesthetics of Death: The Theatrical Elaboration of Ancient Roman Blood Spectacles. *Theatre History Studies* 18 (1998): 89–97.

Humphrey, J. 1986. *Roman Circuses.* Berkeley: University of California Press.

Isaac, James Patton. 1971. *Factors in the Ruin of Antiquity: A Criticism of Ancient Civilization.* Canada: Bryant Press.

Livy. 1926. *History.* Vol. 4. Bks. 8–10. Trans. B. O. Foster. London: William Heinemann.

Saunders, Catherine. 1913. "The Site of Dramatic Performances at Rome in the Times of Plautus and Terence." *Transactions of the American Philological Association* 44:87–97.

Tertullian. 1960. *Apology, De Spectaculis, and Minucius Felix.* Trans. Gerald H. Rendall. London: William Heinemann.

Valerius Maximus. 1892. *Works.* Vol. II. Trans. Conrad Lycosthenis. Paris: n.p.

Vitruvius. 1914. *The Ten Books of Architecture.* Trans. Morris Hicky Morgan. Cambridge: Harvard University Press.

Wiedemann, Thomas. 1992. *Emperors and Gladiators.* London: Routledge.

Flashing Back

Dramatizing the Trauma of Incest and Child Sexual Abuse

Andrea J. Nouryeh

INCEST HAS BEEN a persistent theme in western drama since the Greeks, yet playwrights did not touch the subject of molestation of a child by a parent or other adult family member until the 1970s when the women's movement forced the crimes of domestic violence and rape out of the closet. We now acknowledge that most incestuous relationships are not between consenting or unwitting adults but are exploitations of children whose ages generally range between eight and eleven years old. Female and male survivors of child sexual abuse, who had once been silenced by fear of public humiliation, ridicule, and disbelief, are now encouraged to name the acts that victimized them. As well, the change in public awareness of this endemic and pervasive problem has been reflected in contemporary media, in fiction, and on stage. Two plays written by women—*Getting Out* by Marsha Norman (1977) and *How I Learned to Drive* by Paula Vogel (1997)—give voice to this unspeakable secret. Both playwrights reveal the psychological legacy of incest hidden by family ignorance, embarrassment, and denial. Their plays disclose the effects of trauma on their central characters and force audiences to confront the difficulties of the characters' healing processes.

In *Getting Out* Norman creates Arlene, an undereducated woman in her late twenties who, like at least half of all female inmates in prison, has experienced sexual abuse prior to her incarceration. Her unacceptable survival skills, which led directly to her reform school and prison sentences, have their roots in repeated sexual assaults upon her by her father. According to Dr. Judith Herman, "[F]eelings of rage and murderous revenge fantasies are normal responses to abusive treatment. Like abused adults, abused children are often rageful and sometimes aggressive. They often lack verbal and social skills of resolving conflict, and they approach problems with the expectation of hostile attack. The abused child's predictable difficulties in modulating anger further strengthen her conviction of inner badness" (104).

It is clear from these findings that Arlene's bouts of uncontrollable rage are perfectly understandable, despite the fact that they must be controlled. The institutions in which she has lived for most of her adolescent and adult life have not helped her find alternative problem-solving tools, nor have they provided her with new ways to view herself or the world. Rather, they have reinforced the early childhood trauma. According to the Human Rights Watch Women's Rights Project, "being a woman prisoner in U.S. state prisons can be a terrifying experience. If you are sexually abused, you cannot escape from your abuser. Grievance or investigatory procedures, where they exist, are often ineffectual, and correctional employees continue to engage in abuse because they believe they will rarely be held accountable, administratively or criminally. Few people outside the prison walls know what is going on or care if they do know" (1). Norman shows that Arlene's history as a victim of incest and as a prisoner is a repeated pattern in which she consistently depended for her survival on those who abused her. The psychological impact of these experiences is typical: they have created and reaffirmed feelings of helplessness, vulnerability, loss of safety, and loss of control (Ogdensburg State Mental Facility manual on trauma).

It is telling that Arlene's worst crime, murder, was committed in self-defense during her escape from prison, where she was serving a three-year sentence. No one investigated why she escaped, why she robbed the convenience store, or why she shot the cab driver who had come out of the store's bathroom. Neither did anyone consider the facts: she refused to abort her son Joey in prison because she needed a living being to love; she escaped prison to find him when he had been taken away from her; the man she murdered was a cab driver, like her father; he was also trying to molest her; and the weapon was his own gun, which went off accidentally. Despite these mitigating factors, she was seen merely as an escaped convict and a woman with a history of violent behavior. Consequently, Arlene was blamed for her own victimization. The source of her actions went unexplored; her pleas for help were ignored; and the years of abuse that had trained her to view the intimidation of others as her only viable means for self-protection were compounded.

Arlene was never provided with the counseling that she needed to end this cycle. Instead, she was perpetually robbed of her autonomy. Even the priest who talked to her and gave her an alternative image of herself was sent to her without her request. All she could do to achieve some form of selfhood was to take control by refusing to eat, by lying, by stealing, and by lashing out when threatened. Like most victims of child sexual assault, her coping mechanisms were self-defeating. They encouraged her to regard all relationships with distrust and anxiety despite her need for companionship and acceptance. Her subsequent angry outbursts and vicious attacks on others pushed people further away from her, underscoring her own sense that she was unlovable and wicked. Her early life experiences prepared her to be retraumatized over and over again because she could not trust her instincts. And they reinforced a sense that she was unworthy of help and incapable of changing. That is why she was confronted by memories of the myriad incidents in her past—principals and doctors who did not believe her, guards who taunted her with food and sexual innuendo, female inmates who made unwanted sexual advances—that echoed the initial abuse. It is critical that she never conjured up an image of her father. Instead, the tape of her past life of rape, imprisonment, escape, and ill-fated attempts at survival through theft and prostitution kept playing in her head, intruding on her thoughts because she was looking for answers to the questions: Can I really get out? Am I worthy of a better life? How do I undo the damage and change my life? Whom can I trust? How do I "inherit the earth?"

A parolee on her first day out of jail, she has become a divided self: Arlie, the child, former prostitute, and murderer, who struck out against anyone who tried to interfere with her autonomy over her own body; and Arlene, the submissive Christian and rehabilitated model citizen, whose spirit was broken and whose new identity, given to her by the priest, is based on God's forgiveness for her past sins. The play shows how words and actions create associative memories for Arlene, memories that are reenacted onstage. Over the course of the play, Arlene's fragile and troubled emotional state is revealed through this process of association. The audience witnesses how prison recapitulated her father's abuse and her mother's neglect and further fostered poor self-esteem and antisocial behaviors. They are thus implicated in social service and judicial systems that discredit such victims and deny them the psychological support and the opportunity to learn the appropriate coping skills that they desperately need to become productive members of society.

In *How I Learned to Drive*, Vogel gives us Li'l Bit, a thirty-five- to forty-year-old teacher who serves as both the protagonist and the narrator of the story of her inappropriate "attachment" to her aunt's husband. Having come from an uneducated family (like Arlene), she has managed to get a college education and build a teaching career. Although her family background has not hampered her in terms of her achievements, its ill-informed and contradictory messages about sex are at the root of her psychological struggles. Both the men and the women in Li'l Bit's family were reduced to sexual objects by being given nicknames that specifically referred to genitalia, but only the women suffered if they acted on their desires. They forgave the men for their vulgar and animal-like appetites and accepted that the women's primary role was to cook, clean, and lie on their backs in the dark. They believed that they, as women, had the responsibility to prevent themselves from being exploited by men; that they needed to know how to handle alcohol, prevent pregnancy, and achieve orgasm without much help from their partners. Grandma, a child-bride at the age of fourteen, was picked by Big Papa because she was easy prey: "the plump, slow flaky, gazelle at the edge of the herd" (Vogel 26). She tolerated Big Papa's sexual advances because it was her conjugal obligation, not because she enjoyed them. In fact, her husband was thrilled that she was rather ignorant; it gave him more control. However, this lack of knowledge had its drawbacks. Li'l Bit's mother was forced to marry when she got pregnant in high school—a disastrous marriage that ended quickly—and Aunt Mary married Uncle Peck, a pedophile whom she "enabled" by denying his problem. In a family where shotgun weddings and predatory sexuality were the only frame of reference for understanding "Men, Sex, and Women" (25, 28, 54), Li'l Bit was ill-prepared for the life-lessons that she would learn through bitter experience.

A victim of incest who survived by living two distinctly different existences, Li'l Bit was both the nymphette who spent private time with her uncle, allowing him to touch and kiss her breasts and photograph her in sensual poses, and the overachieving junior and senior high school girl who was alienated from her peers and who refused to dance because she was self-conscious about the size of her chest. Once she went away to college, Li'l Bit became confused and torn apart by her inability to integrate these mutually incompatible experiences of reality (Freyd 19). Gifts and letters from her uncle triggered uneasiness and fear. "[Her] body [knew] things that [her] mind [wasn't] listening to" (Vogel 51). As a result of the sensations that had been unleashed, she had difficulty concentrating, did poorly in school, drank, partied, and obsessed over her troubling relationship with him.

Her uncle's sexual assault was the source of problems related to her body concept, yet the distinct memory of the event had been repressed, denied, and forgotten. According to psychologist Jennifer Freyd, this is a typical adaptive response to betrayal trauma that is associated with

sexual abuse. The memory loss is particularly prevalent when the perpetrator is someone to whom the victim is attached and on whom the
victim is emotionally, and even physically, dependent (Freyd 74). Freyd
further suggests that "the more the victim is dependent on the perpetrator—the more power the perpetrator has over the victim in a trusted
intimate relationship—the more the crime is one of betrayal" (63). In
Li'l Bit's case, Uncle Peck was the only father figure she had ever known.
He listened to her, protected her from her grandfather's outrageous
jokes about her full figure, encouraged her to go to college, and told
her that he loved her and that she was beautiful. Most importantly, he
taught her to drive like a man and take control of her own life by learning to become aggressive, to watch out for others on the road, to survive
accidents.

Through the nonlinear narrative structure of the play, which is composed of flashbacks, Vogel enables the audience to discover, just as the
victim did, the original sexual act that traumatized her central character
at the age of eleven. They bear witness to how Li'l Bit buried this initial
violation in an underlying need for her uncle's love, approval, and attention and demonstrate how her skewed sense of her body robbed her
of a normal adolescent social life. The audience shares in Li'l Bit's confusion about her uncle's and her own desires and emotions throughout
the subsequent years of their relationship up through the point when
she left home for college and forced herself to reject his frightening and
obsessive advances. It is as if the audience functions collectively, like a
therapist, providing Li'l Bit with the opportunity to reconstruct the
history of this relationship and to restore her sense of self by listening
to herself articulate the truth about this past (Herman 1). As bystanders,
caught between her (as victim) and him (as perpetrator), audience members are asked to take sides at the same time that they must feel the
burden of both Li'l Bit's and Uncle Peck's pain (Herman 7).

The central characters of these two plays are drawn in such a way as
to create powerful testaments to the psychological and emotional legacy
of child sexual abuse. In addition, their structures mirror the way rec-
ollections of exploitation and betrayal intrude on the lives of incest survivors. Unlike the verbal linear narratives in which the ordinary memories of most adults are encoded and assimilated into an ongoing life
story (Herman 37–39), Arlene's and Li'l Bit's narratives are fragmentary, filled with disconnected but vivid memory traces. While piecing
together these disjointed vestiges from the past in the presence of a
sympathetic audience—whether another character on stage or patrons
in the auditorium—these women can name, comprehend, and integrate
these incidents into their adult lives.

Arlene, unlike Li'l Bit, always acknowledged the incest but developed a negative self-concept in order to explain why her father continually raped and beat her (Bass and Davis 39). A rehabilitated adult, she wants to forget the past, yet disturbing moments keep resurfacing. She does not tell her story willingly; it is thrust upon her. Outside the fourth wall, the audience is privy to her thoughts. They watch these unwanted memories come alive when they are sparked by sounds, word cues, and gestures. They also observe how her immediate situation hardly differs from anything that she has experienced prior to this first day of parole. Although she wants to focus her attention on the present and on preparations for a brighter future, she is plagued by her own history.

Isolated in solitary confinement in prison, she was desperate to free herself. To do so she became the obedient servant who could be forgiven by society and be worthy of God's love. In a state of hysteria at being abandoned by the priest, the only person who ever listened to her, Arlene literally tried to kill off her angry and hateful self, Arlie, by repeatedly stabbing herself with a fork. Unable to comprehend the priest's metaphoric, biblical language of submission and transformation, she used violence, the only tool she had at her disposal. Yet Arlie did not and could not die, even when Arlene became a model prisoner. Instead, she dissociated, and the self who survived all of the past abuses became split from her. It is this split in personality, represented in the play by two actors embodying the separate selves, that signals Arlene's unpreparedness and inability to survive as a successful and independent adult.

Arriving in her new home, Arlene is bombarded by flashbacks triggered by her interactions with Bennie, the guard who accompanies her; her mother; Carl, her former boyfriend and pimp; and Ruby, her upstairs neighbor. For example, when her mother visits, she calls out, "Arlie? Arlie girl you in there?" (Norman 18). Upon hearing that voice, her childhood name, and that question, Arlene is reminded of the seven- or eight-year-old self clutching her teddy bear on her bed and lying about the bruises to her vagina and thighs that made it difficult for her to walk. Throughout her conversation with her mother, images of Arlie insinuate themselves: her insistence that nobody did this to her, that she had fallen from her bike; her fear of a battering, alcoholic father whose threats forced her to keep silent; and her need for her mother's understanding and comfort (but all she was offered was tea). Her mother's coldness provokes a moment at school when Arlie learned from the principal that her mother wanted her sent away. Mama brings up Arlene's earlier cries for help—her attempting to poison her father when she substituted toothpaste for mayonnaise on a sandwich, her telling a social worker that she had been forced to watch her parents engage in sexual intercourse—but she reinforces the harm that was done by justifying the ongoing neglect or physical beatings that these actions elicited. Still wanting her mother's acceptance despite her insensitivity, Arlene recollects verbally assaulting peers who insulted her mother and physically attacking those whose gossip threatened to uncover the secret of her father's incestuous assaults. These invasive images from Arlene's childhood come crashing in on her and reveal unresolved emotions about her parents. Ignoring their abusive behavior toward her, she, like most incest survivors, has maintained a positive image of her family and continues to seek their approval. It is only when her mother rejects her last attempt at connection that Arlene can acknowledge the extent of her anger and stop expecting the love she never got. "No! Don't you touch Mama, Arlie . . . or eat all Mama's precious pot roast. . . . No, don't touch Mama, Arlie. Cause you might slit Mama's throat" (30–31).

There is no way that Arlene can avoid Arlie's presence in her psyche. Even the bars on her apartment window remind her of her own burglary attempts as an adolescent, and lighting a cigarette prompts her to recall setting herself on fire in an escape attempt. Unsolicited admonitions from Bennie, the guard, about prostitution and his suggestions about taking a bath and needing to eat summon up images of Arlie picking up johns in bars and battling with the sleazy guards who brutally harassed her or tried to force food on her. In response to Bennie's regrets about never having children, Arlene mournfully remembers reciting the cruel lessons she has learned to Joey, the unborn child growing inside her. While Carl tempts her with the money she can make if she goes off with him to New York, she conjures up the dangerous and repulsive encounters with men into which he had forced her and is reminded that it was his forgery of documents that landed both of them in prison.

The audience watches Arlene struggle with her new survival skills as Bennie, her mother, and Carl all engage her with variations on the verbal annihilation and physical coercion that have been the patterns of her life. In each case she finds the language necessary to articulate her feelings and needs and to contain the raw emotion that threatens to erupt at any minute. When mere words prevent Bennie from raping her, Arlene realizes for the first time that she no longer needs to resort to violence in order to protect herself from abuse. From this point on she can confidently say, "I ain't Arlie," and the disturbing reminders of her childhood can fade away (39).

But her healing process is not yet complete. Morning street sounds, wolf whistles and sirens, and the bars on her windows at the start of act 2 continue to invoke the prison cell from which she has just been released. Even offers of help from her neighbor, Ruby, arouse her suspicions of this woman's motives. They remind her of the incident that landed her in a maximum-security cell: she had cracked the skull of an inmate on the bathroom sink when the woman tried to become sexually intimate with her. Although she longs for companionship, Arlene is confused. Her prison experience hardly has prepared her to accept or even comprehend friendship. The women with whom she conversed in prison either left without even a good-bye, or they expected sexual favors. Arlene rarely had anyone to talk to except for the guards and the priest. She never learned how to trust her instincts about who were her friends and, more specifically, who would listen to her, help her sort out her own feelings, and make sound choices.

Toward the end of the play, when she realizes that she has exchanged one kind of prison for another, she despairs about what it really means to have gotten out. Sharing with Ruby the tragic story of her broken spirit and her self-mutilation, she mourns the loss of Arlie. An ex-convict herself, Ruby carefully listens to Arlene's anguish and comforts her in a manner that no one ever did before, with real empathy and without judgment. She is even able to protect Arlene while allowing her autonomy, and to encourage her to forgive herself for trying to annihilate the child within her—the child who had helped her survive. Spurred by this display of sisterhood and hope, Arlene confronts Arlie again, but this time they share a laugh over a childhood prank. At that moment her transformation is assured: she has begun to heal and to accept this former self as an integral part of her life's story.

In *How I Learned to Drive* we, the audience, participate in the play, learning only as much as Li'l Bit is willing to tell, rather than having access to her inner thoughts and private encounters. She is our driver-education teacher, like Uncle Peck was hers, and addresses us directly: "Sometimes to tell a secret, you first have to teach a lesson" (Vogel 9). Her story is told through flashbacks that surface randomly, moving back and forth in time, a common phenomenon for incest survivors who have yet to retrieve the buried truth. Vogel uses a voice-over that explains when the narrative is shifting in and out of reverse, when it is idling in neutral, and when it is moving forward through first, second, and third gears. Although these memory traces seem yet to be organized and integrated into her personal history, it becomes evident that Li'l Bit has already taken control and has put in place the fragmentary traces of the abnormal and seductive relationship with her uncle (Herman 37). She articulates them in this disordered manner in order to teach us the lesson, to draw us into her feelings of confusion, desire, and betrayal. Our experience then becomes visceral. We undergo a revelation of the secret at the root of her troubled adulthood in a manner that approximates her own. It is only when the shocking moment of trauma is revealed that the resonances across seven years of memories can be felt and the nature of Uncle Peck's abuse can take on its full meaning. In this play we, not the protagonist, are the ones who will be transformed by the end of the narrative.

The metaphor of the driving lesson is crucial; it is both the beginning of Li'l Bit's abuse and the means by which she is able to break the cycle. However, we do not learn this until the penultimate moment of the play. Instead, we are taken on a road tour of scenes between Li'l Bit and her family, her peers, and her uncle that become increasingly more unnerving as they zigzag back and forth across the years from summer 1962 until December 1969. Periodically, Li'l Bit stops to "idle" in neutral, to turn off in a digression that provides the audience with crucial background information, or to share insights she has gained since rejecting her uncle's love.

It is imperative for us to comprehend how Li'l Bit dealt with her confusion throughout her adulthood. Like many incest survivors, she was conflicted by disquieting sensations brought on by her in-body memories. She tells us how she responded to these effects of childhood trauma through alcohol abuse, promiscuity, self-destruction, and suicidal ideation. She was kicked out of school, had trouble holding down jobs, and refused to go home for holidays until after Uncle Peck had died. She knew that his presence was dangerous to her and that she had to renounce his psychological, emotional, and physical hold on her, but she wasn't clear about the reason. In 1979, ten years after confronting him for the last time, Li'l Bit reenacted the early seduction scenes of her adolescence by taking a young high school student back to her hotel room. In the dark she thought of Uncle Peck and tried to comprehend what had transpired between them: "oh—this is the allure. Being older. Being the first. Being the translator, the teacher, the epicure, the already jaded. This is how the giver gets taken" (28). At that point in her history she had yet to uncover the hidden secret and was still trying to figure out why her uncle had become obsessed with her and why she felt both guilty and betrayed.

Later in the narrative, Li'l Bit allows us to be addressed directly by Aunt Mary, who speaks to us as if we were her confidantes in 1969. She tries to convince us that Peck is a good man who struggled with alcohol and improper desires. Although she has some inkling about her husband's pedophilia ("I wish you could feel how hard Peck fights against it—he's swimming against the tide, and what he needs is to see me on the shore, believing in him" [44]), she is more comfortable blaming Li'l Bit and being jealous than protecting her niece from him. Yet despite suspicions about her niece's designs on Peck, Aunt Mary is in such denial that she continues to push them together. When Li'l Bit storms out of the house, angry at her family's crassness and lack of respect for her privacy, we see her aunt insist that Peck go after her: "You're the only one she'll listen to when she gets like this. . . . Peck's so good with them when they get to be this age" (15).

It is the playwright, more than her protagonist, who wants us to hear this perspective on the interactions between the uncle and niece. Because Aunt Mary seems to be the injured party, her views, although decidedly biased against Li'l Bit, shed light on their encounters and call the audience's responses into question. The first scene Li'l Bit enacts for us illustrates this. It is the summer of 1969. Seventeen and seated in the front seat of a car, she talks suggestively to the married man beside her and then allows him to unhook her bra and fondle her breasts. Only when she becomes uncomfortable at the sensation his kisses elicit does she rear back and stop him: "Uncle Peck—we've got to go. I've got graduation rehearsal at school tomorrow morning. And you should get on home to Aunt Mary—" (12). With that moment Vogel throws the audience off balance. This is not just any January-May romance, and the playwright hasn't given us enough information to judge who is more to blame for the relationship, Uncle Peck or Li'l Bit. In this way we seem to be primed to side with Aunt Mary, as we see Peck's caring devotion and witness Li'l Bit's flirtations. One can only imagine that if Li'l Bit had discovered the secret of her uncle's sexual assault and confronted her family (and her audience) with it at that point, no one would have believed her.

We become even more confused about guilt or innocence when Li'l Bit takes us back to the summer of 1968, when Uncle Peck escorts her to an inn to celebrate her driver's license. Although he has sworn off alcohol in her presence, he plies her, a minor, with martinis and gets her drunk. Despite her inebriated state, she realizes that there is something distressing about this assignation: "What we're doing. It's wrong. It's very wrong. . . . It's not nice to Aunt Mary." Peck snaps back, "[Y]ou let me be the judge of what's nice and not nice to my wife" (22). It is quite evident that he has rationalized his clandestine evenings with his adolescent niece when he insists that no one will get hurt. After all, he believes he hasn't forced her to do anything and has already assured her that "nothing is going to happen until [she wants] it to" (23). But it is clear from his question, "do you want something to happen?" that he hopes eventually she will agree to consummate their relationship (23). We, the audience, become even more perturbed when her reply, "I don't know," prompts his predatory response: "[T]hen I'll wait. I'm a very patient man. I've been waiting for a long time. I don't mind waiting" (23). This is underscored when Peck grabs a lap rug from the back seat and Li'l Bit shouts out fearfully, "What? What are you going to do?" (23).

While digesting the implications of this scene, we witness Uncle Peck teaching Cousin Bobby to fish for pompano. Here Li'l Bit seems to be sharing corroborating evidence she used to help her deal with the truth and with her feelings about her own complicity in her victimization. Although it is not explicit—we never see the little boy—we come to understand that Uncle Peck will molest him in some way. When Bobby cries about killing the fish, his uncle comforts him: "I don't want you to feel ashamed about crying. I'm not going to tell anyone, okay? I can keep secrets. You know men cry all the time. They just don't tell anybody, and they don't let anybody catch them. There is nothing you could do that would make me feel ashamed of you" (23–24). He seals this bargain with an idea for a picnic of beer and crab salad to be eaten in an old, hidden tree house; but he insists that "it is a secret place—you can't tell anybody we've gone there—least of all your mom or your sisters—this is something special just between you and me" (24). We can infer that the seduction of drinking illegal beer and having private time with this older, wiser man in his "special place," along with the promise that Uncle Peck will protect the secret of his unmanly crying, works its charm on Bobby.

In this way we are confronted with examples of Uncle Peck as a manipulator and exploiter of children. Given two major pieces of evidence, we can begin to assess how Li'l Bit was psychologically coerced into an inappropriate liaison by the man whom, until these moments, she seems to have "twisted around her little finger" (44). Later, therefore, when Aunt Mary actually addresses us, we can no longer be satisfied nor agree with her version of the relationship between Peck and Li'l Bit because we cannot excuse his abuse of power as an adult.

Over the course of the play, Li'l Bit shows us how, before ever teaching her how to drive, Peck took advantage of her sensitivity and her need for a father. From the time she was twelve years old she noticed his drinking and his "bad spells" and made a deal with him: to meet once a week and talk about things that were bothering him as long as he didn't drink. These meetings would be secret. She would say that she was studying with a girlfriend. Tellingly, she insisted that these meetings be in public: "You've got to let me draw the line. And once it's drawn, you mustn't cross it" (46). We do not know the reason behind this condition, but when we hear it, we have already witnessed that, within a year, Peck has managed to cross that line without any objections from her.

A prematurely developed thirteen-year-old girl, Li'l Bit spent Saturdays alone with him in his basement, willingly posing for him in front of his camera like a pornographic model. Despite her outrage at his suggestion that these photo shoots were in preparation for a portfolio to submit to *Playboy* magazine (thus putting her on display by the time she would be eighteen), he placated her with promises of secrecy and a declaration of his love. We recall her insisting, at the beginning of the scene, that there would be "nothing showing"; yet by the end of the photo session, she was unbuttoning her blouse. Thus we perceive how she had betrayed her initial desires by her own actions and how Peck had successfully seduced her into compliance with his adult fantasies and wishes. He had transformed her into his ideal woman, who, like a car (what Li'l Bit calls "a Boy's First Love"), was "someone who responds to your touch—someone who performs just for you and gives you what you ask for" (34).

The secret to which she alluded at the beginning of the play continues to lurk beneath the surface of the scene of Li'l Bit's first official driving lesson in 1967. It is in her line, "but then I'm locked in with you," her smart retort to Peck's "make sure all the doors are locked" (33). It is there again when he admonishes, "I never want to see you driving with one hand. Always two hands," and she suggestively replies, "if I put my hands on the wheel—how do I defend myself?" (33). Compared to his seriousness of purpose, her flippant remarks seem playful, coquettish, and filled with sexual overtones. Yet her questions are quite genuine. Although she may not be conscious of the reason, she cannot believe him when he says, "I will never touch you when you are driving a car" (33). Now fifteen or sixteen, Li'l Bit is old enough to hear the secrets of defensive driving and self-preservation that she needs as a woman. By teaching her the skills of thinking "what the other guy is going to do before he does it" (34), Peck, her surrogate father, finally is showing her how to protect herself not only from others but from him. But this lesson has come too late. He had already victimized her five years before.

This is the horrible secret that has to be told. In 1962, on the back roads of the Carolinas when she was eleven years old, Peck had molested her. It was her first unofficial driving lesson. Because it was illegal to let her take control of the steering wheel, he was able to swear her to secrecy. She could not reach the pedals, so she was seated on his lap. He would push the gas and the brakes while she steered the car. As she placed her two hands on the wheel, he held her closely against him with his two hands on her chest. She relaxed in his grasp and asked, "[A]m I doing it right?" (56). Suddenly, he accelerated and slipped his hands under her blouse onto her budding breasts. Terrified, all she could do was plead for him not to continue and, as he ejaculated, to tell herself, "[T]his is not happening" (56). Li'l Bit ended this revelation with an explanation: from that day on she stopped living in her body.

The first time Li'l Bit held on to the steering wheel of a car, she was too young to put her life in her own hands. Yet this is what she insisted on doing. In response to her mother's reluctance about letting her travel alone with Uncle Peck, she argued that she could handle him. Rejecting her mother's protests that her uncle paid far too much attention to her and looked at her in an improper manner, she claimed that these fears were all in her mother's head. She pleaded, "I still deserve a chance at having a father! Someone! A man who will look out for me" (55). Rather than put her foot down and protect her daughter from the inevitable, her mother allowed her to prevail, but she admonished her with a warning: "[I]f anything happens, I hold you responsible" (55). This was Li'l Bit's sentence: to bear the brunt of the responsibility, to feel that she had betrayed herself, that she had let down her guard and jeopardized her own safety, and there would be no one with whom she could share her pain. How could she have told her mother what had happened? How could she have admitted it to herself? She hadn't heeded her mother's premonitions and Peck had sworn her to secrecy. Needing him in her life and incapable of believing what he had done to her, she dissociated and stored the event deep in her subconscious. It took nearly twenty-five years for her to discover that it was not her fault—that it was the adult who was supposed to have watched out for her—not the other way around.

Both Marsha Norman and Paula Vogel have written plays that illuminate the experiences of those who have been victimized by incest and child sexual abuse. Using the technique of flashbacks that are achronological, they illustrate opposite ways in which children learn to deal with their molestation, reveal the patterns of obsession with the past and of memory retrieval that are characteristic of adult survivors, and explore the various effects these traumas have had on their self-concepts and interpersonal relationships. Yet these plays ultimately ask very different things of their audiences.

Getting Out is a realistic play that foregrounds the "apparatus of stage realism—the proscenium arch, the details of set, and so on"—as a theatrical metaphor for "the cultural confinement of women" (Schroeder 138). Distanced beyond the fourth wall, we are voyeurs who have access

not only to what takes place in Arlene's life on parole but to her recol-
lections of the past. We are thus enabled to comprehend the personal
and social problems that have led to her imprisonment and subsequent
release. Although this may, as Patricia Schroeder suggests, "challenge
the values encoded and disseminated by a patriarchal culture, . . . and
simultaneously support the alternative values—such as economic autonomy and female community—that feminism espouses," it allows us a
kind of emotional safety (142). Unless we too are child abuse survivors
or former prison inmates, we are able to leave the theatre reassured that
Arlene has found new ways to deal with the legacy of her father's abuse.
We are comforted that she has learned to reject prostitution, to control
her rage, and to trust a friend.

How I Learned to Drive, on the other hand, refuses to let the audience
off the hook so easily. We are not allowed by the conventions of realism
to remain passive, albeit empathic, observers. Rather we are participants
in a rhetorical lesson that the narrator has prepared for us. Like in a
Greek tragedy, we are tossed between protagonist and antagonist and
are asked to take sides. There is even a Greek chorus—the schoolmates
and family members—that comments on and interprets the actions that
are depicted and forces us to confront our own musings and doubts
about the characters' guilt or innocence. Thus, we must take stock of
the reactions we have had to the victim, Li'l Bit, and the perpetrator,
Uncle Peck, throughout the narrative. We know that Peck's pedophilia
has had catastrophic consequences and that no one has remained un-
scathed. On the other hand, we were led to believe in his goodness and
his love for his niece. Perhaps we even blamed her for his obsession.
Once the secret is unearthed, however, we, like our narrator, have to
make sense of the memory fragments. We, like Li'l Bit, have been betrayed by Uncle Peck and can do nothing to undo the trauma nor prevent its aftershocks. At the end of the play, Li'l Bit addresses us directly
and informs us that she has learned to forgive, but we know that she
will always be scarred. We also know that child sexual abuse is cyclical
and that the perpetrator is often someone who was also abused as a
child. We wish we had had the opportunity to intervene or, at least, like
our narrator, hear the answers to her questions: "Who did it to you,
Uncle Peck? How old were you? Were you eleven?" (Vogel 54). Rather
than leaving the theatre reassured, we harbor an unsettling feeling that
perhaps we had judged Li'l Bit too hastily, that perhaps we had been
too easily taken in by Uncle Peck, and that perhaps we are somehow
implicated, not only in her victimization but in the exploitation of all
children by adults.

Works Cited

Bass, Ellen, and Laura Davis. 1994. *The Courage to Heal*. New York: Harper-Collins.

Freyd, Jennifer J. 1996. *Betrayal Trauma: The Logic of Forgetting Childhood Abuse*. Cambridge, Mass.: Harvard University Press.

Herman, Judith Lewis. 1992. *Trauma and Recovery*. New York: Basic Books.

Human Rights Watch Women's Rights Project. 1996. *All Too Familiar: Sexual Abuse of Women in U.S. State Prisons*. New York: Human Rights Watch.

Norman, Marsha. 1979. *Getting Out*. New York: Dramatists Play Service.

Ogdenburg State Mental Facility. n.d. Untitled manual on trauma.

Schroeder, Patricia R. 1996. *The Feminist Possibilities of Dramatic Realism*. Madison, N.J.: Fairleigh Dickinson University.

Vogel, Paula. 1997. *How I Learned to Drive*. New York: Dramatists Play Service.

The "End" of Violence

in Northern Ireland

Gender, Dramaturgy, and the
Limits of Aristotelian Form

John Countryman and Charlotte Headrick

I N A SPEECH DELIVERED shortly before his untimely death in
November 1988, Belfast playwright Stewart Parker remarked that

> writing about and from within this particular place [Northern Ireland]
> and time [since 1969] is an enterprise full of traps and snares. The raw
> material of drama is overabundant here, easy pickings. Domestic bickering,
> street wit, tension in the shadows, patrolling soldiers, a fight, an explosion,
> a shot, a tragic death: another Ulster play is written. What statement has
> it made? That the situation is grim, that Catholics and Protestants hate
> each other, that it's all shocking and terribly sad, but that the human spirit
> is remarkably resilient for all that. (Muinzer 48)

Philomena Muinzer has described the same condition as "the merry-
go-round of violence" (52).

There is evidence that the conventions of "Aristotelian" form have
exacerbated the sectarian violence in Northern Ireland by provoking a
dramaturgical merry-go-round that perpetuates the political. Many of
the so-called Troubles plays (those associated with the violence in the
North) and the actual violence itself (construed as a dramaturgical/
theatrical phenomenon) subscribe to the principles of Aristotelian or
"classic" form. At the same time, there is evidence that gender is a factor
in the construction of violence, both figurative and real.

These arguments rest on a reconsideration of the familiar dramaturgical conventions associated with Aristotle's *Poetics,* in particular, the
importance for the integrity of Aristotelian form of a resolution, an
"end" to events that constitute the "beginning" and "middle" of the

drama. Participants in the Northern Ireland conflict have adopted a fatalistic view of events in the region. They perceive the violence as somehow inevitable and endemic because, among other things, they have internalized the Aristotelian model of action, which is arguably a model of events (both artistic and real) accepted uncritically, even unconsciously, by almost everyone in Western culture. It encourages us to seek or to impose "narrative closure" on events—what Frank Kermode has called "the sense of an ending." Historiographer Hayden White has argued that narrative closure produces a "tidy ending" not only in the formal sense but in a moral sense as well (5–17).

In both Northern Ireland and contemporary society in general, this "script" is no longer appropriate. In previous generations the myth of martyrdom attached to those who died as a consequence of political violence (which, it seems, compelled combatants to compose their actions in accordance with narrative form) was successful precisely because political violence was associated with the mystique of sacrifice and cultural renaissance. Aristotelian form is no longer an enabling or ennobling design for political action in the context of today's Ireland, however, because it now suggests that there is not nor will there ever be any sort of permanent resolution to the problem, only an endless chain of incidents whose "end" is merely the beginning of a new round of violence. This phenomenon fuels the sort of cycle of retribution and revenge associated with the *Oresteia* but, we hasten to add, without the presence or convenient "vehicle" of a scapegoat who can, in the spirit of René Girard, bear responsibility for the violence and break the cycle once and for all.

In general, male playwrights in Northern Ireland (Brian Friel, John Boyd, and others) have adopted Aristotelian form and have thereby unwittingly affirmed a model of action that has become in the minds of its adherents as much a fact of nature as a principle of aesthetics. Their decision to do so has almost certainly exacerbated the conflict or at least has offered no new approach to the problem. In a sense they have applied a linear approach to a circular phenomenon, when an episodic or Brechtian approach would have been more appropriate.[1] Episodic form and the devices of "epic" theatre identified with Brecht serve to reveal the discontinuities in a conflict and to accommodate the complexities and ambiguities of a dramatic situation, even if this means suggesting that no "resolution" (i.e., narrative closure), in the Aristotelian sense,

---

[1]Although Aristotle asserts that only a poor playwright would arrange incidents episodically, obviously dramatists no less accomplished than Shakespeare have done so.

is possible. This has been the approach adopted by many of the female dramatists who have composed "Troubles" plays in recent years.

Our examination of the violence itself and of selected play scripts that have both prefigured and reflected that violence reveals an alternative to the male-oriented "eye for an eye" scenario that Aristotelian dramaturgy has spawned. This is an alternative dependent upon the assumption of an altogether different dramaturgical model—one that encourages dramatists from the North to move beyond identification with events, beyond uncritical acceptance of the status quo, and toward critical analysis and constructive action. Such discovering or creating alternatives to prevailing structures, Marilyn French argues, is exceedingly difficult because the

> present social and political situation provides us with no imaginable alternative. . . . We choose the status quo . . . since any act may entail something worse than the present situation.
>
> But if we decide actively to oppose patriarchal values, we find no clear direction. For our system incarnates patriarchal values [and] as long as our institutions are hierarchical, power remains supreme. Yet, because power is indeed supreme, no alternative structure is as successful in our world.
>
> New structures can emerge successfully only in response to a new or different set of ends. (494–95)

The "ends" in this case, of course, are not resolutions but goals. As scholar Angela Bourke eloquently asserts:

> We have urgent need of stories in Ireland at the moment, as our society comes to terms with painful memories [and] with twenty five years of violence in Northern Ireland, followed by the sudden possibility of peace, and then more violence; and with a heartbreaking series of revelations about betrayal of trust, about domestic violence, and about cruelties secretly inflicted on women and children. The old narratives will no longer serve, and it is not just politicians and journalists who are struggling to make sense of it all. Religion used to offer answers and explanations, but more and more it is artists who confront the broken certainties that lie all around. The literature and oral tradition of the Irish language were used for so long in the service of self-righteous patriarchal nationalism that for years the most creative and radical minds in the country wanted nothing to do with them. But that is changing. . . . More and more, as silenced voices speak, the need for different kinds of language is being acknowledged. (305–6)

We would argue that the alternative endings that the women of the North have forged is the sort of "new language" to which Bourke refers.

In his book *Contemporary Irish Drama* Anthony Roche discusses Christina Reid's *Tea in a China Cup*. Among other things, he considers the relevance of Julia Kristeva's essay "Women's Time" to a full appreciation of the play. Kristeva argues that historical time is "linear time" and suggests that it is exceedingly difficult to reconcile "maternal time (motherhood) with linear (political and historical) time" (Roche 231). Roche writes that "if male linear time constitutes a history, it is a written history and one that writes reproduction out of the record," and he notes that Kristeva "posits an alternative women's time, in which there are 'cycles, gestation, the eternal recurrence of a biological rhythm which conforms to that of nature' " (231). Roche goes on to apply this theory to Reid's play, a play in which the cycle of male history attempts to submerge the female cycle. He contends that in Reid's play "women's experience is asserted against history, against a narrative of absence and death" (232).

William Demastes continues the argument. In his book, *Theatre of Chaos,* he reflects that the reason contemporary writers have difficulty with closure is their "resistance to tidy, self-contained traditions of classic realism and naturalism," and he quotes Sam Shepard, " 'Endings are so hard. Because the temptation always is a sense that you're supposed to wrap it up somehow. You're supposed to culminate it. . . . And it always feels so phony' " (117). These playwrights, Demastes continues, are "intuitively aware of the scientific fact that information exists in an orderly state (the only kind that permits comfortable closure) only in systems rarely existing in the natural world itself. As twentieth-century science began investigating dynamic systems, the implicit closure of the [Aristotelian and] Newtonian paradigm[s] could no longer be located. Nature itself has proved to be dynamically open-ended. Similarly, strictly linear, causal, realist theatre has begun to give way . . . to drama that attempts to reveal the indeterminate, open-ended, and chaotic nature of the world" (117). Furthermore, as Katherine Hayles points out, "chaotic unpredictability and nonlinear thinking . . . are just the aspects of life that have tended to be culturally encoded as feminine" (173).

Jeanie Forte, in fact, advances this point, arguing persuasively that a traditional realist play may not also be a feminist play because classic realism supports the dominant ideology. "In writing practice, then," Forte continues, "a refusal to perpetuate the conventions of realism/ narrative would presumably not only thwart the illusion of 'real life,' but also would function to threaten the patriarchal ideology imbedded in the 'story.' A subversive text would not provide the detached viewpoint, the illusion of seamlessness, the narrative closure, but instead would open up the negotiation of meaning to contradictions, circularity, multiple viewpoints; for feminists, this would relate particularly to gender" (117).

Anne Devlin writes that her *After Easter* was an attempt to "recapture my Mother's universe" and that when she writes, she thinks "in terms of birth. Work is always like maternity. Creativity is like birth. I believe that you inherit your mother's and grandmother's consciousness" ("Group discussion" 1995). When asked by the Royal Shakespeare Company if she could write a play with "lots of women's parts," her response was "yes, yes, yes! In the 1980s, I was very conscious of feminism and terrorism, and I asked myself, 'Why am I not a terrorist?' " ("Group discussion" 1995). She has also remarked that had she remained in Belfast, she would have become a terrorist like her character Josie in *Ourselves Alone*.

Roche argues that central to feminist theatre is an "even-handedness in the dramatic representation" (238–39). In many plays from the North, as well as from the Republic, there is not a single Aristotelian protagonist. What we have are clusters of women who share the stage. This is true for Devlin's *Ourselves Alone* (1986) and *After Easter* (1994), Marina Carr's *The Mai* (1994), Reid's *Tea in a China Cup* (1983) and *Joyriders* (1986), Marie Jones's *The Hamster Wheel* (1990), and Charabanc Theatre Company's *Somewhere over the Balcony* (1987) and *Lay Up Your Ends* (1983). These plays—in their rhythms and structure, which reflect "women's time," and in their emphasis upon a collective image of women rather than a singular heroine—defy Aristotelian strictures.

Just as these scripts reflect "women's time" in their collective portraits of women, the lack of closure in the scripts also depicts women's experiences in the North. We would argue that the violence in the North leads to a lack of closure in the scripts. This absence of closure questions the status quo. In fact, the plays of Carr, Devlin, Reid, Jones, and of Charabanc Theatre Company are replete with the effects of violent acts, both large and small, acts that Brendan Kennelly calls "emotional murder" (Pine 22).

An example of this violence is found in Christina Reid's *Joyriders*. Reid's play begins with a group of teenagers watching a production of O'Casey's *Shadow of a Gunman* (a typically "Aristotelian" play), and Reid's nod to O'Casey is clear throughout the play. Maureen and Sandra of *Joyriders* are enrolled in a Youth Training Programme in Belfast. Naive, sweet Maureen is killed when "she run between the car an' the army" (Reid 63). Christopher Murray sees in Maureen an echo of O'Casey's Minnie, noting that, "like Minnie Powell, Maureen is caught in the crossfire" (Murray 191).

In a scene that precedes Maureen's death, Reid includes a telling stage direction. She opens the scene with the sound of glass being swept up. She writes in the stage direction, "[T]his is the sound that usually follows violence in Belfast" (Reid 52). Maureen's broken body reminds us of the sound of the broken glass—the memory of the sound fore-shadowing yet another violent death. Sandra, Maureen's friend, sees Maureen's death in a clearly pragmatic way: "It's not lovely, an' it's not romantic like in stupid friggin' plays!" (63).

Despite the 1995 cease-fire, long since broken and reestablished, and despite the 1998 vote for peace in the North, every few weeks there is another report of another incidence of violence in Northern Ireland.[2] The people of the North sweep up the broken glass, but as Reid's Sandra already knows, the reality of life in the North has no tidy ending like a "friggin' play," and she, like the real girl on which she is based (and others like her), lives with uncertainty and open endings.

Unless they are writing fantasy, women writers in the North find it difficult at best to find closure and resolution in a world that has neither. In Aristotelian terms resolution means that the audience should come to a new understanding of itself and the world, or as one critic phrased it, it should "be able to provide answers to unanswered questions" (Barranger 63). More often than not, however, resolution merely confirms our assumptions and affirms an existing state of affairs.

In the *Poetics* Aristotle called for a clear resolution to the action, but just as the women in "real life" Belfast cannot find a resolution, the world they create on stage, which is fraught with violence on several levels and of several types, does not contain endings, peaceful or otherwise. Often, the audience is left "hanging," in limbo, a situation akin to their daily lives. The women's world onstage and off is a world where "things" are never quite finished. Accordingly, their drama is filled with examples of characters whose lives are "hanging" and unfinished. Christine in *Christine* and Karen in *Twinkletoes*, both written by Jennifer Johnston and published as *Three Monologues*, are excellent examples. Christine's husband is dead and Karen's husband, Declan, is in prison. Neither woman has achieved resolution by the end of her respective monologue. Violence not of their own making has shattered both of their worlds: Christine's Billy is shot by the IRA; while Karen's husband has been imprisoned for IRA activity. Christine has suffered a kind of

---

[2]Since this paper was presented in April 1998, three Catholic boys died the week of 5 July in a senseless fire bombing during the Protestant "marching season" in Northern Ireland and a number of churches were burned in retaliation. On 15 August 1998 twenty-eight people died in Omagh in a car bombing that also injured 220. Of the twenty-eight who died, seven were children. Three generations of women in one family also lost their lives. Clearly, there is no closure in the North.

abuse at Billy's hands. Unable to become pregnant, Christine lets Billy, for the whole of their married life, think it is her "fault": I never had the heart to tell Billy what they said at the hospital. . . . I just let him think it was my fault. . . . You know the way some men are. . . . [T]hey get very hurt about that sort of thing, ashamed. That's why I never told him the truth. It was hard sometimes not to let it come bursting out . . . you know, when we had a wee row or something (*Christine* 51).

Although from different worlds, Protestant Christine and Catholic Karen share a mutual pain, and each makes a sacrifice that is a tiny act of violence to her person. Christine gives up her beloved Church of Ireland for Billy's Presbyterianism and endures the hardship of Billy's elderly father living with them. Karen longs for a life. In her late thirties, she wants another child, wants to dance, wants to be free (whatever that may mean); but she is in the limbo that is the lot of a wife of an IRA prisoner. If she had an affair, her husband would be informed, and reprisals might occur; but living without him is an earthly purgatory. Her husband's history of violent acts continues to inflict pain in the present. Karen muses:

> I want to have more kids.
> I want to love.
> Not just on Thursdays.
> Aye, Declan, I love you.
> I lie well.
> You've fucking well ruined my life, Declan.
> That's what
> I want to say.
> And your own.
> You're a hero.
> Wear it well, I say. (*Twinkletoes* 29)

At the end of the play Christine is moving out of her home, leaving for an unknown world, and there is no closure. At the end of *Twinkletoes,* Karen is left in the same state of limbo. All that has changed for both women is that the audience has witnessed their pain.

Many of the women playwrights in both the North and the Republic have received negative reviews or, worse, no attention at all. Some have not even published because their plays are not Aristotelian. Anne Devlin's plays (especially *After Easter*), for example, have been described as messy and disjointed, and Sarah Hemming of the *Independent* says of *After Easter* that "it is a rich, complex and unsettling piece, but also muddling and unsatisfying. . . . Threads are picked up and dropped summarily—bold writing: irritating watching" (399). Carole Woddis defends the play, which "may be flawed and barely joined at the middle. But it is also a pungently witty, poetic and painful attempt to make discernible the indiscernible" (699).

Clearly, because life in the North is often both messy and violent, the mess and the violence spills over into the writing of the women who attempt to depict that life and chronicle the vicissitudes of the North in their dramas. As a consequence, women writers have struggled to find new ways to deal dramaturgically with the violence. Rejecting classic Aristotelian models, many of these women opt for a looser structure, for monologues, for open-ended plays that may be artistic attempts to reflect the chaos around them. Open endings can leave audiences disturbed, ill at ease, tense. As a character in one play blurts, "[W]e've been an occupied country for centuries now, and you wonder that I'm a little tense" (Jirges 23).

The stories of Christine, Karen, Greta (in Devlin's *After Easter*), and Ethel in Marie Jones's *Ethel Workman Is Innocent* leave us wondering what will happen next. Certainly Jones's Ethel leaves us wondering how she has been changed by her brush with the Other (literally the other side), her Catholic darts competitors. Although it is a comedy, *Ethel Workman* has a dark undertone, as we see Ethel's brutish, working-class/Orangeman/Presbyterian husband forbid her to participate in her much loved darts tournament. Marina Carr's *The Mai* introduces us to three generations of women, a matriarchy that is functioning quite satisfactorily until the Mai's husband, Robert, who had abandoned her and the family, decides to return. His male presence disrupts the household, unleashing the rage that leads to the Mai's suicide—a kind of closure, perhaps, but a violent and unsettling resolution at best.

Without exception, violence, both mental and physical, is an integral component of these plays just as it was in the tragedies of ancient Greece. In Euripides' *Medea*, the title character suffers deep psychic violence. She is a woman in pain, having sacrificed everything for Jason, and consequently she is betrayed when Jason abandons her for another woman. Medea's pain is akin to Greta's in Anne Devlin's *After Easter*. Greta's Oxford don husband is having an affair; she may or may not be in the throes of postpartum depression; and no one believes her visions of flames and fire, visions which, in fact, may be the way that she escapes her isolation and copes with her husband's violence toward her. All of the women in Christina Reid's *Tea in a China Cup* have been abandoned, wounded by men. So too have the women in Marie Jones's *Somewhere over the Balcony*. Abandoning a pregnant woman is an act of violence just as surely as physically beating her up, and abandoning one's children is a common act of violence in play after play by women writers in both the North and the Republic. These plays then are peopled by women who have been subjected to violent acts: the violence of abandonment, physical harm, or mental abuse.

Playwright Brendan Kennelly was inspired to write his version of *Medea* after spending time in St. Patrick's Psychiatric Hospital in Dublin, where he was recovering from severe alcoholism. He found himself surrounded by women, many of them abused. He writes, "I found myself listening, listening especially to women. . . . Many of them had one thing in common. Rage. Rage mainly against men, Irishmen like myself" (6–7). Critic Jane Edwardes believes that Kennelly's *Medea* succeeds precisely because of his understanding of the central character, an understanding that resulted from his talking to the women in the hospital. Edwardes describes these patients as women who "had cracked after a lifetime of oppression and were consumed with rage. Kennelly was passionately drawn to such women. Perhaps they reminded him of the tinkerwoman he saw being stoned when he was only four" (Edwardes 929). In a later interview Kennelly speaks of "emotional murder." He sees his *Medea* in those terms: "I was surprised that nobody picked that up, in terms of politics, in terms of emotional murder, that people do kill—maim and kill—emotionally around them; it's very strong in Dublin pubs, the way we emotionally assassinate each other" (Kennelly, in Pine interview 22).

What the men do to the women in Reid's *Tea in a China Cup* and what happens to the women in Johnston's *Christine* and *Twinkletoes* exemplify a form of violence that is tantamount to emotional murder. Emotional murder is also at the heart of Anne Devlin's *After Easter*. Devlin paints with broad brush strokes. Her play is nonlinear, and episodes are loosely connected. Beginning and ending with surreal monologues, the play assumes a circular pattern. There is no clear path ahead for the heroine, no decisive future, and at the end loose threads are left dangling.

In writing the play Devlin said she sensed there would be one of two events in her country: peace or civil war. In her attempt to meet brutality with humanity, she wrote *After Easter*. Greta, the lead character, is in the process of finding her way back from madness. She has left Northern Ireland, married a Protestant Englishman, and as a consequence is a stranger in a strange land, simultaneously trying to understand her past, adapt to the present, and work toward a future.

Greta's visions drive her to speak to her cousin Bethany, a nun. Frustrated with her conversation with Bethany, Greta commits if not a violent act certainly an antisocial one (although in her mind it is an act of Reconciliation). She steals a chalice filled with communion wafers and distributes them to people in bus queues. She is arrested, and her sister Helen convinces the police to release Greta: "I told them she'd been in a mental hospital in England and was out for a week because her daddy was in the Royal with heart trouble. So when I confirmed that she was just nuts they were happy to let her go. . . . In England they lock her up if she's mad but let her go if she's political. In Ireland they lock her up if she's political and let her go if she's mad" (*After Easter* 47). Her sister Aoife responds to Helen, "[D]o you think Greta's mad?" and Helen retorts, "[N]o more than anyone else in this country" (47). These lines echo conversations from the beginning of the play in which Greta argues with her doctor that she is not suicidal: "Look, if I sat down on the road with twenty people I'd have been arrested. Because I sat down on the road on my own it was a suicide attempt. Confirms what I've always suspected—the difference between insanity and politics is only a matter of numbers!" (3).

Greta realizes that her first vision of fire is an image of Pentecost, when the flame of the Holy Spirit is visited on the disciples. She dreams of fire and tells of how at a dinner party her hair actually caught on fire. When Helen has a vision, it also involves light: "Wings and eyes of light were falling through the rooms" (74). The images of flames recall the fire of battle, heating by fire to strengthen, being burned to be purified, and, most important, being possessed by God to perform some great task. Greta's self-immolation is violence, but it is violence of a very strategic kind. Ancient monks flogged themselves to purify their soul, a violent act that was meant to assure moral cleansing. Buddhist priests burned themselves to death in protest of the Vietnam War. Greta has suffered violence at the hands of her husband, her father (whose ghost literally tries to pull her into his coffin), and England. She is visited by heavenly violence, the visions that torment her. Devlin might argue that virtually all of the violence in the play is designed to purify. But what Devlin (through Greta) argues for is a sociological and political cleansing that will bring an end to the violence of everyday life in Northern Ireland.

At the end of the play the audience finds Greta rocking the baby from whom she was estranged. Devlin thus uses one of society's most powerful images to send a message of reconciliation and healing, forged from everyday acts of "emotional murder." Although the play "ends," it has no closure. We see Greta with her baby, but we really do not know how she got to this point nor where this moment will take her.

Devlin wrote her play during the first historic cease-fire in 1994, and the poignant moment at the "end" of the play is symbolic of what is to come. Devlin hoped at the time that peace would prevail, but the cease-fire has since been broken and violence and counterviolence continues in Northern Ireland. There is no resolution. We still have questions, and there are no answers.

Greta's madness is a metaphor for the violence of the North, and Greta's struggle to heal is Devlin's hope for her own country, her own time, her own generation. Greta's madness, manifest in her messy life and the multiple threads of the play, are metaphors for the "whole of Ireland." Although arguably her madness was triggered by the mental abuse she endured from her English husband, her teaching colleagues, and the insensitive English who surround her, she *is* Ireland, and her madness is the dysfunction not only of one individual but of a divided country as well.

Sociologically, psychologically, and politically, the violence on the streets of Belfast and other communities in the North leads inevitably to a drama of the unresolved in which violence in all of its many guises is portrayed both onstage and off and for which, until a lasting peace is found, there can be no closure.

Works Cited

Aristotle. *Poetics*. 1968. Trans. Leon Golden. Englewood Cliffs: Prentice-Hall.

Barranger, Milly S. 1990. *Understanding Plays*. Boston: Allyn and Bacon.

Bourke, Angela. 1997. "Language, Stories, Healing." In *Gender and Sexuality in Modern Ireland,* ed. Anthony Bradley and Marianne Gialanella Valiulis. Amherst: University of Massachusetts Press.

Demastes, William. 1998. *Theatre of Chaos*. Cambridge, UK: Cambridge University Press.

Devlin, Anne. 1991. *Ourselves Alone*. In *Contemporary Plays by Women*, ed. Emily S. Kilgore. New York: Prentice-Hall.

———. 1994. *After Easter*. London: Faber and Faber.

———. 1995. Group discussion with cast of *After Easter*. Stratford-upon-Avon. 21 January.

Edwardes, Jane. 1989. *Time Out*, 17 July. In *London Theatre Record* 9, no.15:929.

Forte, Jeanie. 1989. "Realism, Narrative, and the Feminist Playwright: A Problem of Reception." *Modern Drama* 32 (March): 115–27.

French, Marilyn. 1985. *Beyond Power: On Women, Men, and Morals*. New York: Ballantine Books.

Girard, René. 1977. *Violence and the Sacred*. Trans. Patrick Gregory. Baltimore: Johns Hopkins University Press.

Hayles, N. Katherine. 1990. *Chaos Bound: Orderly Disorder in Contemporary Literature and Science*. Ithaca: Cornell University Press.

Hemming, Sarah. 1995. *Independent*, 5 March. In *London Theatre Record* 15, no. 7:399.

Jirges, Lorilyn. 1993. "The Troubles." Unpublished manuscript.

Johnston, Jennifer. 1995. *Christine*. In *Three Monologues*. Belfast: Lagan Press.
————. 1995. *Twinkletoes*. In *Three Monologues*. Belfast, Lagan Press.
Kennelly, Brendan. 1991. *Medea*. Newcastle-upon-Tyne: Bloodaxe Books.
Kermode, Frank. 1967. *The Sense of an Ending*. New York: Oxford University Press.
Lattimore, Richard, trans. 1953. *The Complete Greek Tragedies: Aeschylus I: Oresteia*. Chicago: University of Chicago Press.
Muinzer, Philomena. 1987. "Evacuating the Museum: The Crisis of Playwriting in Ulster." *New Theatre Quarterly* 3, no. 9:44–63.
Murray, Christopher. 1997. *Twentieth Century Irish Drama: Mirror Up to Nation*. Manchester, England: Manchester University Press.
Pine, Richard. 1992. "Q & A with Brendan Kennelly." *Irish Literary Supplement* 9, no. 1 (spring): 21–23.
Reid, Christina. 1987. *Joyriders*. In *Two Belfast Plays*. London: Methuen.
Roche, Anthony. 1994. *Contemporary Irish Drama: From Beckett to McGuinness*. Dublin: Gill and Macmillan.
White, Hayden. 1973. *Metahistory: The Historical Imagination in Nineteenth-Century Europe*. Baltimore: Johns Hopkins University Press.
Woddis, Carole. 1994. *What's On*, 8 June. In *London Theatre Record* 14, no. 11:699.

The Fallacy of Contextual

Analysis as a Means of

Evaluating Dramatized Violence

J. D. Martinez

WITH THE ADVENT of the "mass media," conventional dramatic methods for depicting violence have become significant factors in contributing to the increase of aggressive and antisocial behaviors in the world's industrial societies. The latest studies verify this assertion and also point to serious ethical concerns. Because the standard techniques used to arouse an audience emotionally through the representation of violence on television and in movies (the so-called mass media) were derived originally from the live theatre, the artists who initially created and established these conventions share a moral obligation to expose those that may encourage negative psychological and sociological effects. Given today's "climate of violence" and the results of recent studies, scholars and artists can no longer hide behind arguments that "adjusting" the context of violence portrayed by the media ameliorates negative effects of that violence.

In any study of staged violence, a brief history of the phenomenon is instructive. It is common knowledge that historically the dramatization of violence has been a staple of the performing arts. Evidence exists, for example, to support the theory that, prior to what is usually considered the origin of the western theatrical tradition in ancient Greece, depictions of violent acts were incorporated into rituals performed by primitive peoples. Cesare Molinari, in *Theatre through the Ages,* offers the example of the Yahgan of Tierra del Fuego, who, "to celebrate a funeral, staged a mock-battle [in] which each side accused the other of having been, directly or otherwise, the cause of the death of the deceased" (4). Most of the extant early Greek theatre tragedies contain scenes of death and physical violence. Although the Greeks placed these scenes offstage, the results of the violence were frequently presented in graphic tableaux *onstage.*

Violence became more prevalent as an onstage action in the Greco-Roman theatre and even more so in the sanguinary theatrical spectacles in the Roman amphitheatres and other representations of violence in full view of the spectators that continued into the Middle Ages. In the Medieval era, a great deal of graphic violence (e.g., a detailed portrayal of the Massacre of the Innocents, complete with blood effects and dismembered bodies in *The Death of Herod* within the *Ludus Coventriae*) occurred on stage in religious dramas. Also familiar are the graphic scenes of violence in the Shakespearean and Jacobean theatres; the physical rough-and-tumble, knock-about performance style of the commedia dell'arte; the "flamboyant" violence of nineteenth-century melodrama; and the extravagant excesses of the Grand Guignol. Thus, such graphic contemporary representations of violence as the carving of an ear in Martin McDonagh's *The Beauty Queen of Leenane* occupy a place in a long-standing and firmly entrenched theatrical tradition.

Considering the central position violence has occupied in the theatre and its popularity with audiences, it is hardly surprising that scholars, dramaturgs, and performing artists would advance the argument that any negative effects of viewing violence can be diminished or eliminated by the creation of the proper context. In *Violence in Children and Adolescents* Richard Sparks, teacher of Criminology at Keele University, argues that not all TV violence is equally detrimental because it is "something that occurs in a setting of some kind; in television its position in a narrative designedly holds certain significances; narratives made up of stylistic devices conventionally mark their action as realistic or fantastical, serious or comedic or whatever; all of this is further interpreted by viewers in light of their own needs and desires, assumptions, skills and so on" (139). These arguments, which emphasize context, thus support the continued depiction of dramatized violence and its dramatic necessity.

In his introduction to *Violence in Drama* Thomas Gould, professor of Classics at Yale University, supports this view and laments that "a person who counts great drama and serious literature as indispensable sources of pleasure is likely to listen with mounting dismay to arguments against the portrayal of violence. To be deprived of the killing of Hector, the suicide of Ajax, [or] the blinding of Gloucester would be intolerable. . . . Most lovers of literature hope that . . . a distinction can be made between right and wrong kinds of violence, between 'essential' and 'gratuitous' violence" (1).

Although Dr. Gould's nostalgia is understandable and his argument compelling from a sociological point of view, he fails to demonstrate how an audience's making the necessary distinction might be ensured. In fact, it is of little consequence to make distinctions between "essential" and "gratuitous" acts of dramatized violence because both seem to have the same effect on their audiences.

The United States, the nation with the highest homicide rate in the developed world, has seen violence soar to epidemic levels over the past several decades. It is not coincidental that we are also the world's foremost producer of violent programming. During this explosion of actual violence on our streets, we have also witnessed an explosion of dramatized violence on our screens. This apparent correlation between entertainment violence and the rising crime rate has engendered a passionate outcry from the general public and an ongoing debate about whether there exists a causal relationship between media violence and actual aggression. For the medical, public health, and scientific communities, however, the debate is over. They agree that a causal relationship indeed exists between media violence and aggression.

Extensive study has led researchers to conclude unequivocally that the mass media contributes significantly to the aggressive behavior and attitudes of many children, adolescents, and adults. Of the two meta-analyses conducted, the first (Andison 1977) examined sixty-seven studies and over thirty thousand subjects; the other (Hearold 1986) surveyed 230 studies and close to one hundred thousand subjects. These analyses yielded two significant conclusions: first, there is a strong correlation between exposure to televised violence and aggressive behavior over a wide range of ages and measures of aggressive behavior; and second, exposure to violent programming not only increases aggressive behavior but is associated with lower levels of prosocial behavior.

These findings were corroborated by a 1982 National Institute of Mental Health report: "In magnitude, television violence is as strongly correlated with aggressive behavior as any other behavioral variable that has been measured" (3). The American Psychological Association (APA) subsequently endorsed the National Institute of Mental Health conclusions that televised violence has a causal effect on aggressive behavior. The APA joined other professional groups—such as the American Medical Association, the American Academy of Pediatrics, and the American Academy of Child Psychiatry—in endorsing this finding. And finally in

1993, after forty years of denial, even the television networks publicly acknowledged that the viewing of dramatized violence contributes to aggressive behavior and that access to violent programming should be restricted (Chen).

Thus, the debate is over; the relationship is clear. Viewing dramatized violence is indeed a significant contributing factor in fostering violent behavior. Making distinctions between "essential" and "gratuitous" violence or seeking to evaluate violence as appropriate or inappropriate, good or bad, right or wrong according to its context is absurd from a sociological perspective. Attempts to contextualize violence—which depend on processes such as reason, judgment, or intellectual assessment—are irrelevant because the arousal effects caused by viewing dramatized violence do not depend on such cognitive processes.

It may be useful at this point to explain how dramatized violence (specifically that in film and television) is crafted when the express purpose is to evoke an emotional response from a viewer. To arouse someone with a violent act, the artist must establish a sense of anticipation and a sensory receptivity to violent actions *prior* to presenting the act of violence itself. In other words, the artist's aim is to create a vulnerability in the viewer. This vulnerability is perhaps better defined as a receptive "mood"—an inclination, a state of mind, a pervading impression. Creating a receptive mood in the viewer, then, is half the battle in controlling the viewer's emotions. Once a spectator is "in the mood for violence," context (the reason for the existence of violence) becomes almost immaterial.

Most people can be easily influenced by what they see and hear once the proper mood has been created. For example, soft candlelight and a woman's gentle voice can readily turn a young man's thoughts to romance. Once he is in a romantic mood, the young man is more susceptible to suggestions of intimacy and tenderness. Soft candlelight and a woman's gentle tone of voice can also be used by TV producers to elicit a particular response from TV viewers. In other words, media artists can use the same kind of emotional cues we respond to in real life to establish a specific mood for (and in) their viewers. In theatre, television, and film these "cues" are stimuli that are consciously or unconsciously perceived by the viewer, and they act as signals for (or actually elicit) a change of mood in the spectator. Any type of mood can be created by setting up the appropriate cues. For example, the candlelight and the woman's gentle voice cue the TV viewer that this is a romantic scene.

Whereas sensory cues that educe a romantic mood are "lovely" and benign, cues that cause a mood for violence are not. Emotionally disturbing sensory cues used in the construction of scenes of dramatized violence can remain with the viewer for a long time. In one of the earliest studies of media comprehension, researchers Holaday and Stoddard (1933) discovered that scenes with the most dramatic visual and auditory cues were more likely to be recalled than less overtly dramatic scenes. More recently, psychologists Calvert and Watkins confirmed these results (1979).

Many standard cues are used by directors to generate specific moods. These cues or tools (what the semioticians among us might call "signs") are derived from theatrical conventions, such as music and lighting, that have been recognized for generations and passed from artist to artist by word of mouth and through example. TV and film directors use these cues to manipulate the viewer toward a visceral response to dramatized action.

Most violent scenes in theatre, television, and film have a beginning (a setup), a middle (a climax), and an end (a release of tension). All three parts are essential for the violent scene to achieve the desired emotional effect on the viewer. When sensory cues are added to this structure to create a dramatized act of violence, a viewer's efforts to contextualize at the moment of witnessing such an act are futile.

The beginning of a violent scene (the setup) is usually cued by a change in background music. Music is one of the principal means of creating a mood, and it reinforces the other "mood-cues" in a scene. The music may be soft and tender, as in a love scene, for example, or loud and exciting, as during a car chase. Imagine how turning off the sound while watching a car chase on TV would diminish the overall impact of the visual images. A change in music, then, is what sets up the change of mood. To cue the spectator that something violent is about to happen, the music may become suspenseful or strange, or the music may increase in tempo and volume. These changes cause feelings of anticipation, perhaps anxiety, in the viewer.

Artificial lighting is another common tool used to manipulate a viewer's emotions. Lighting in television and in film, as well as on the stage, is always artificial. Even daylight scenes filmed outdoors are enhanced with artificial lighting, which can be manipulated in a variety of ways. In the beginning stages of a scene of violence, for example, the lighting may change along with the background music. The scene may become suddenly dark and shadowy, which creates a feeling of suspenseful anticipation in the viewer. Will someone or something suddenly jump out at the victim from a dark shadow? It is the *contrast* between light and dark that creates the anxiety, and it is along that edge of contrasting light and dark that the visual threat of violent action (the knife, the gun, the monster's claw) often emerges. The director may also change the color of the light. Frequently, unusually saturated colors are used to cue spectators that they have entered a strange and potentially dangerous environment.

Near the middle of a scene of violence, the director wants the spectator to feel more tense and anxious. An increase in tension generates more intense feelings of suspense and anticipation in the viewer, a response that can be enhanced by a sudden change in the music, lighting, or more often, by a rapid shift in an audience's point of view (POV), which is accomplished by changing camera angles. Every viewer's visual POV is carefully anticipated, and thus everything he or she sees on the screen is chosen in painstaking detail. Nothing is left to chance. For example, the film director or camera operator will decide exactly what image the TV viewer will look at, how long the viewer will look at that image, and how often the viewer's POV will be changed.

As we get closer to the violent action itself (the climax of the scene), the camera angles shift abruptly. The viewer's POV may be yanked from a close-up on a character's frightened face, to a long shot of a dangerous environment, to an extreme close-up of a vicious-looking weapon, then back to the victim's face again. These shifts produce an unsettled, almost disoriented, feeling in the viewer. By artfully combining the sequences of a number of highly effective cues, the director is able to manipulate the viewer into the "right" mood, create emotional vulnerability, and render the viewer receptive to the possibility (and the occurrence) of violence.

This manipulation is particularly important in the climax in a scene of violence that revolves around the physical acts themselves. In a fast-paced act of violence, loud sound effects, screams, and so forth complement the visual image. The audience's POV (identical to the camera's) is manipulated at an ever-increasing tempo, and spectators are made to watch every gory detail represented. The camera shifts swiftly from a weapon of destruction, to a fist smashing an innocent face, to the gruesome injury inflicted, to the reactions on the victim's face, or to a close-up of a bloody wound. Throughout this sequence the spectator is subjected, often subliminally, to wild, frenetic music and powerful lighting effects. Orchestrated chaos! Poeticized violence!

But let's backtrack a bit. Long before the violent action, the audience has been seduced (if the director and the actors are skillful) into identifying emotionally with the victim and into feeling animosity for the attacker. The viewers are made to care about the characters in the story (i.e., to identify with them on some level) so that the act of violence itself will achieve an even greater emotional impact.[1] The exploitation of an audience's identification with characters has been crucial to the dramatic experience for hundreds of years. For many theatre artists the notion of identification with characters is allied with a transferal of emotional response from actor to audience. Eighteenth-century critic and playwright Joseph Addison referred to the idea of audience identification with a character as a "secret comparison which we make between ourselves and the person who suffers" (2: 149). In *Creating a Role* Konstantin Stanislavski stated that "actors can fill whole auditoriums with the invisible radiations of their emotions" (106). And Bertolt Brecht, in *A Little Organum for the Theatre,* defined identification as "Einfuhling," or empathy (17).

Thus, to an overwhelming extent an audience member's response to dramatized violence is visceral. The viewer is not afforded time to think, to be critical, or to reflect. During the act of violence itself, for a few vulnerable moments, he or she is transfixed. Reason and judgment are halted in a classic "suspension of disbelief." The viewer simply reacts emotionally to the carefully constructed, sequential stimuli. The acts of violence themselves are drained of meaning and context. In short, the spectator is not allowed to consider *intellectually* the consequences or significance of what is happening on the screen. He or she has been manipulated emotionally by experts into a "mood for violence," manipulated into hoping that violence will occur or perhaps into hoping that it won't occur. In either case the viewer is already engaged in a dramatic "ritual of arousal."

As the violent scene ends the viewer is gradually introduced to a new set of cues that assist in releasing tension. It is important that the audience member be allowed to rest emotionally for a few moments. Therefore, the music, artificial lighting, violent sound effects, and quickly

---

[1]Of course, it is just as easy for an artist to reverse the usual archetypes and convince an audience that it should hate an evil Victim and cheer for a violent, aggressive Hero. A viewer's inclination to identify with a dramatic character can be exploited in many ways. In a paper delivered at the biennial meeting of the Society for Research in Child Development in 1991, psychologists Hendrix and Slaby reported that adolescent boys and girls are equally susceptible to the effects of TV violence and tend to identify with the character of the same sex as themselves. Unfortunately, exploiting gender stereotypes in aggressor/victim relationships in violent programming is painfully prevalent. This is part of a larger issue concerning the essential qualities of victim and victimizer and their traditional roles in the construction of dramatized violence that I haven't the space to adequately address here.

shifting camera perspectives all subside, and the viewer is given a moment to dwell on his or her feelings for the characters and to relive what has just transpired. Then it all begins again.

Of course, none of these processes is wholly new. As a fight choreographer and researcher on historic methods of stage combat for over twenty-five years, I have no doubt that Shakespeare's company used many of the same kinds of techniques to emotionally arouse its audiences. And yet I wonder how much violent theatrical entertainment the average person witnessed in the seventeenth century? Citing an A. C. Nielsen Company Report on television viewing habits, the American Academy of Pediatrics reported that the *average* child has watched five thousand hours of TV by the first grade and nineteen thousand hours by the end of high school. During those thousands of hours of television viewing, the typical eighteen-year-old has witnessed two hundred thousand acts of violence, including forty thousand murders.

Despite repeated claims of "cathartic" effects of viewing televised violence advanced by senior executives of the broadcast industry from the 1960s to the 1980s, virtually no evidence exists that watching aggression enables children to release "pent-up" hostility, anger, or rage. In fact, just the reverse is true. A study by researchers Comstock and Paik (1990) has identified and documented the following consequences of viewing violence: the aggressor effect—increased mean-spiritedness, aggressive behavior, and even serious violence toward others; the victim effect—increased fearfulness, mistrust, and self-protective behavior toward others; the bystander effect—increased callousness, desensitization, and behavioral indifference toward real-life violence among others; and the increased appetite effect—increased desire to view more violence.

Given the irrefutable causal relationship between viewing violence and its negative psychological and social effects, it is unthinkable for artists to continue to justify the dramatic portrayal of violence by making distinctions between essential and gratuitous violence. To be fair, it must be acknowledged that violence in the media is not the sole reason that our society suffers from an epidemic of violence. Nevertheless, it is an incontrovertible contributing factor. If the importance of enacting violence at all is to instruct and enlighten (as Dr. Gould intimates) and not merely to illicit emotional arousal, then in order to minimize those arousal effects, theatre and media artists must avoid exploiting the powerful theatrical techniques that create visceral responses to dramatized violence. In the past it was theatre artists who taught television and film directors how to exploit an audience's vulnerabilities. Perhaps fittingly, it falls to theatre artists to fashion a creative bulwark against that exploitation, to challenge contextualization as the means of rendering violence harmless, and to expose the hazards of dramatized violence.

Works Cited

A. C. Nielsen Company. 1990. *Nielsen Report on Television.* Northbrook, Ill.: Nielsen Media Research.

Addison, Joseph. 1868. *The Works of Joseph Addison.* Vol. 2. New York: Harper & Brothers.

Andison, F. Scott. 1977. "TV Violence and Viewer Aggression: A Cumulation of Study Results." *Public Opinion Quarterly.*

Anonymous. *Death of Herod, Ludus Coventriae.* 1468. Cotton MS Vespian DVIII: British Museum.

Brecht, Bertolt. 1951. "A Little Organon for the Theatre." Trans. Beatrice Gottleib. *Accent* 1:13–40.

Calvert, Sandra L., and Bruce A. Watkins. 1979. "Recall of Television Content as a Function of Content Type and Level of Production Feature Use." Paper presented at the meeting of the Society for Research in Child Development, San Francisco.

Chen, Milton. 1990. *The Smart Parent's Guide to Kid's TV.* San Francisco: KQED Books.

Colvard, Karen, and Joel Wallman. 1995. *Report of the Harry Frank Guggenheim Foundation.* New York: Harry Frank Guggenheim Foundation.

Comstock, George, and Haejung Paik. 1990. "The Effects of Violence on Aggressive Behavior: A Meta-analysis." Unpublished report to the National Academy of Sciences Panel on the Understanding and Control of Violent Behavior, Washington, D.C.

Donnerstein, Ed, Ron Slaby, and Leonard Eron. 1986. *The Development of Aggression in Children of Different Cultures: Psychological Processes and Exposure to Violence.* Chicago: University of Illinois at Chicago.

———. 1993. *The Mass Media and Youth Aggression.* Washington D.C.: American Psychological Association.

Eron, Leonard D., Jacquelyn H. Gentry, and Peggy Schlegel, eds. 1994. *Reason to Hope: A Psychological Perspective on Violence and Youth.* Washington, D.C.: American Psychological Association.

Gould, Thomas. 1991. *Themes in Drama.* Vol. 13, *Violence in Drama.* Cambridge: Cambridge University Press. 1–13.

Hearold, Susan L. 1986. "A Synthesis of 1043 Effects of Television on Social Behavior." In *Public Communication and Behavior,* ed. George Comstock. Vol. 1. San Diego: Academic Press. 66–133.

Hendrix, Kate, and Ronald G. Slaby. 1991. "Cognitive Mediation of Television Violence Effects in Adolescents." Paper presented at the biennial meeting of the Society for Research in Child Development, 18–20 April, Seattle, Washington.

Holaday, Perry Ward, and George D. Stoddard. 1933. *Getting Ideas from the Movies.* New York: Macmillan.

Huesmann, L. Rowell, and Leonard D. Eron, eds., 1986. *Television and the Aggressive Child: A Cross-National Comparison.* Hillsdale, N.J.: Lawrence Erlbaum.

Molinari, Cesare. 1975. *Theatre through the Ages.* London: Cassell & Company.

National Institute of Mental Health. 1982. *Television and Behavior: Ten Years of Scientific Progress and Implications for the Eighties, Summary Report.* Washington, D.C.: National Institute of Mental Health.

Singer, Jerome L., and Dorothy G. Singer. 1981. *Television, Imagination, and Aggression: A Study of Preschoolers.* Hillsdale, N.J.: Lawrence Erlbaum.

Slaby, Ronald G., Wendy C. Roedell, Diana Arezzo, and Kate Hendrix. 1995. *Early Violence Prevention, Tools for Teachers of Young Children.* Washington, D.C.: National Association for the Education of Young Children.

Sparks, Richard. 1977. "Television and the Well-being of Children and Young People." In *Violence in Children and Adolescents,* ed. V. Varma. London: Jessica Kingsley.

Stanislavski, Konstantin. 1961. *Creating a Role.* Trans. Elizabeth Reynolds Hapgood. New York: Theatre Arts Books.

Listening to the

Language of Violence

The Orchestration of Sound and Silence
in Fights for the Stage and Screen

Dale Anthony Girard

THE IDEA OF LISTENING to the language of violence is one that frequently conjures up images of foul words, screams, and yells of hate and fury. There is, however, a great deal more that is distinctive about the language of violence. In contemporary film and theatre the language of violence must contain every sound (or silence) presented in a fight sequence. This includes not only the thump and "pow" of the actual fight but also the sounds of the weapons, armor, costumes, props, set, crowd, and combatants themselves. Yet, its importance notwithstanding, there has been little integration of the concept of orchestrating sound and silence into the production of violence on the dramatic stage. In the four most recent publications on the art of staged conflict (Girard, *Actors On Guard*; Hobbs, *Fight Direction for Stage and Screen*; Martinez, *The Swords of Shakespeare*; and Suddeth, *Fight Directing for the Theatre*), for example, the language of violence is barely addressed. Three of the four manuals mention the topic and acknowledge the importance of sound, but a detailed examination of the how and why is generally neglected. In response to the need for a comprehensive treatment of the subject, this article will therefore present a point-by-point overview of the language of violence and will define the proper orchestration of sound and silence in fights for the camera and the dramatic stage.

Sounds of the Silver Screen

The reception of cinematic violence is not as simple an act as it may appear. In viewing violence on both the contemporary stage and screen, spectators tend to look principally at the act—i.e., at the image and its effects. That, however, may not be sufficient, for much of the dramatic impact derives not from the image presented but from the sound that supports that image. This explains why people find a particular piece of filmed violence captivating only to discover how little impact the sequence actually has when they turn the sound off. This and similar experiments demonstrate how dependent audiences have become on the language of violence in comprehending the story being told.

Ever since the silver screen converted to "talkies," production teams have striven to add dynamic sound to the action taking place in front of the camera. More recently, the creation of the proper sounds necessary for physical encounters has become such an integral part of film and television production that a specific specialty—that of the foley artist, a specialist who recreates the sounds of movement and other sounds in a recording studio after a film has been shot—has been developed (Singleton 68). Within the controlled environment of their studio, the foley artist and the sound effects technician "manipulate" every sound to be included in a film, attempting to create the exact sound needed to accompany every act or action of the fight sequences. Through the use of computers and digital recording, pitch (the relative "highness" or "lowness" of a particular sound); rhythm (the temporal pattern produced by the grouping and balance, or conversely the imbalance and unpredictability, of sounds and dialogue during a fight); duration (the length of time for which a sound or silence is sustained); volume (the magnitude of a sound); quality (the essential character or distinguishing attributes of a sound); and intelligibility (the identification and clarity of a sound and its ability to convey a certain meaning, emotion, or message) are controlled precisely (Raphael, 1:12–15). Such control of these elements, however, is something that cannot easily be transferred to the stage. Consequently, the fight director in the theatre must take the time to listen actively to the language of violence within staged fights.

Knowing What You Hear

The "conditioning" of today's movie audiences through sound makes the believable presentation of stage violence considerably more difficult. Even with highly trained actors, countless hours of rehearsal, and a flawless performance, without the addition of sound audiences most likely would respond to a staged fight with incredulity. They would witness the fight, subconsciously compare that experience to expectations conditioned by film and television fights, and most likely leave the theatre dissatisfied. For modern spectators believability is determined by the plausible representation of what seems to be actually occurring.

A fight onstage, however, is not intended to be real in a strict sense. Rather it is intended to move the plot forward, saying what needs to be said about the characters and their circumstances in a way that the audience can accept and understand. In a real fight sound is the "sloppy" by-product of the immediate physical action. Onstage it cannot be so. Sound, as much as any other part of the production design, is necessary to tell the story effectively. Therefore, ignoring the sounds of physical conflict at a critical moment in a production can destroy communication and the meaning of a particular dramatic moment, confuse an audience, and decrease the emotional impact of the scene.

Vocal Orchestration

The actor's voice is the common element in both stage and screen performance. It is the one variable controlled, at least to a certain extent, by the actor. Whereas pitch, duration, volume, and quality of the voice are generally related to the specific activities of the fight, rhythm (and to a lesser extent volume) is an independent, artistic variable. Changes in breath, sound, silence, and delivery of lines can make a critical difference in a fight's presentation. During a stage fight, however, the essential characteristics of the actor's voice can be lost (or at least muted) unless they are carefully orchestrated with the other sounds of conflict, much the way they are in the movie sound studio. Consequently, the actor must remain aware of how he or she is using the voice, while simultaneously conveying the feelings, thoughts, emotions, and clarity of imagination experienced by the character being portrayed.

To avoid misleading or misinforming the audience, both the actor and the fight director must focus on the full spectrum of natural vocal sounds within a fight. Finding the natural vocal sounds of a fight involves significantly more than simply developing a "grunt-per-move ratio." Rather it involves exploring sound patterns that reinforce the movement of the fight. It is imperative then that the sounds be "character specific," not actor specific. These sounds come from the world of the character, much like a specific dialect or physical mannerism. Character-specific sounds thus fully support the activity, situation, and circumstances of both the character and the conflict.

Vocal Sounds

There are generally two types of vocal sounds within a fight: voluntary and involuntary. Voluntary sounds are those that the combatant releases by choice and include lines of dialogue; aggressive, threatening chatter; challenging, taunting sounds; and intentional moments of silence. All voluntary sounds result from intention or desire, not accident. Because of this, voluntary sounds generally emanate from the aggressor. They are more predictable and controlled than involuntary sounds and can vary widely in pitch, volume, and quality. Because voluntary sounds are controlled by the character, they generally consist of a combination of closed and open sounds, with consonants used to break up the open vowel sounds, which produces a "logical" series of sounds.

In contrast, involuntary sounds are reactive, resulting more from accident or impulse than from the conscious exercise of will. Involuntary sounds include the natural sounds of the working body and include grunts, groans, sighs, and other unintentional phonations on exhalation. They can also be reflexive responses to unexpected stimuli such as wounds to the body, hard physical contact, startling or aggressive actions by an opponent, or anything that catches the combatant by surprise. Because they are reactive, involuntary sounds generally come from the victim. Because these sounds are unpredictable, spontaneous resonances not subject to control of the will, they tend to exhibit a great diversity in pitch, volume, and quality. And because these sounds are quick physical responses, the sounds produced are generally open and possess instinctive, primitive qualities.

Within the structure of the fight, it is important to find the contrasts between voluntary and involuntary sounds and to explore their many variables. Through an understanding of the nature of the sound (whether active or reactive), the actor develops a better and more dynamic presentation of a character in conflict.

Reactive Physical Vocal Range

In a perfect world all sounds would be "organic" (truthful to the action being presented); unfortunately, the world is less than perfect, and not all sounds can be organically created. For example, an actor cannot react organically to a cut wrist if no cut exists nor to a blow to the stomach or a sword in the chest if these actions have not actually taken place. The "involuntary" sounds generated by these actions, which are produced naturally in the real world, then, must be created voluntarily in the theatre. For this it is important to understand the "reactive physical vocal range," the correspondence between the relative vocal pitch and the part of the body being attacked.

Like the ringlets undulating from a stone dropped in a pond, the vocal register of the voice rises by degrees. The lowest vocal register starts at the body's physical center, around the diaphragm, and builds in pitch outward from that point. When we stub our toe or receive a paper cut on a finger, the involuntary sound emitted is in our higher vocal register; but when we are struck in the stomach or hit in the crotch (both men and women), the pitch drops. Simply put, as the stimulus for the involuntary sound moves away from the center, the pitch rises; conversely, as the sound moves closer to the body's center, it becomes lower in pitch.

It is interesting to note that the reactive physical vocal range is used quite differently in comedy—what might be called *The Comic Inversion*. One of the basic techniques of comedy is to establish a particular pattern, and then to break it, thereby subverting the realistic effect. Comic inversion in stage combat, then, is the process of offering contradictory vocal reactions to real and believable physical injuries. Cartoons provide perhaps the best examples of this process when they show characters who, when hit in the head with a frying pan or anvil, emit a slow, deep vocal response. Other characters may react with a sharp, high pitch when kicked in the groin, and still others may not respond at all on being hit hard in the stomach. Contrasts and/or reversals established by a performer's seemingly inappropriate reaction to a hit can be quite humorous if used selectively and unpredictably.

Depicting an Injury

Depicting an injury presents unique problems for the actor. When a person is injured, he or she emits an involuntary sound at the time of impact; but that is not the sole effect of the injury. Continued or specific movement can aggravate the wound: the beating of the heart can cause it to throb, loud sounds can cause an injured head to ache, heavy costumes or armor can further injure a bruised or battered body, and so on. All of these can generate involuntary sounds that result from pain. The pitch of the sound generated is determined by its location on the body; its volume and duration depend on the intensity of the hit; and its quality and rhythm (generally most evident in breathing and vocal patterns established after the injury) depend on the nature of the wound.

Again, although the actor's reactions may not be "real," they must appear real and must remain truthful to the action. It is important to find the "correct" vocal response because every member of the audience has in some way experienced and heard the involuntary sounds of pain. If the sound chosen is not truthful, the audience will recognize the falsehood (if only on a subconscious level), and this recognition will invariably diminish the effectiveness of the fight. Correctly and skillfully developed vocal orchestration, on the other hand, can create the illusion of spontaneity and real danger.

Playing the Pauses

So far in the process of isolating and controlling the vocal sounds in fight orchestration, the focus has remained on sounds in response to specific actions and reactions, not upon the sounds of inaction. Between the actions, activities, beats, and phrases of a fight, there are moments of rest. These, however, are not necessarily moments of vocal rest. In other words, the effects of any injury sustained can still be heard, the fear and tension of the characters may be audible, or the characters' physical strain and fatigue might be heard in the rhythm and sound of their breath. During these breaks in the physical action the tension generated by what has come before must be sustained and must carry the listener into the next sequence of action. The sounds during a pause in the action should "summarize" the previous action and should inform the audience who is in control, losing control, out of control, or being controlled. They are therefore frequently bridges to a greater understanding for the audience.

Vocal Variety

As the voice is explored and used within the fight's orchestration, it is important to remain aware of the differences and similarities in the actors' voices. Differences render them distinctive in the orchestration, whereas similarities allow them to blend with other voices. To best emphasize each actor, the fight director must strive for the greatest difference in sound, while remaining aware of the demands of character and circumstances. If the combatants sound too much alike, the intelligibility of the story diminishes because of the loss of clarity about who is being affected and in what manner. Hence, the actors' voices must differ enough in pitch, rhythm, volume, and quality to allow the audience to identify characters' actions and reactions by sound as much as sight.

The Sound of Impact

In addition to the actors' voices, the orchestration of a fight consists of the sounds of body against body, fist to flesh, bone on bone. Such sounds are essential to a fight because they convey not only that contact has been made but the strength or degree of that contact as well. Whether these sounds are created manually or mechanically, they must create the impression of truth. Like the reactive physical vocal range described earlier, the sound of impact on the body has a different pitch depending on the part of the body being attacked. Similar to vocal reactions, contact made to the center of the body generates a lower pitch than a blow made to a limb or to the face. As contact moves away from the physical center, the pitch of the blow rises.

In orchestrating a fight this factor is significant. The wrong sound at the wrong time can create the impression of a "fake" fight, destroy the illusion the director has constructed, and seriously damage the story being dramatized. If the intention is to show the truth of a character's circumstances and the causal relationship between actions, the sounds of those actions must match the expected sounds. Sound for sound's sake or inappropriate sounds can distance an audience from the world of the play as quickly as a poorly choreographed or poorly executed fight sequence.

Knapping the Blow

In the studio the desired sounds of impact can be created easily, but in the theatre it is considerably more difficult to achieve believability because actors onstage generally must create the sounds themselves as they perform the fight. These self-made sounds of impact are known as *knaps*. The term is used to represent the various ways in which a combatant can safely create the sound of a punch, stroke, blow, or kick in order to heighten the illusion of violence. Knapping can be achieved in a number of ways: by either combatant clapping his or her hands together; by light contact of one combatant's hand, foot, or fist with a designated muscle group on the other fighter; by the combatants striking each other's hands; or by a fighter's slapping muscle groups on his own body. Knapping can even be accomplished by someone else onstage. Not only do these techniques keep the trick hidden from the audience, but they also provide the fight director with much-needed variations in the pitch, duration, volume, and quality of the overall sound of the fight.

Foleying the Fight and Sound Effects

Not surprisingly, technology has made both the actor's and the director's jobs easier. Multitrack digital recorders, compact disks, and digital keyboards used in some theatres today do for the stage what the foley artist has done for film. With small speakers strategically placed around the set and an arsenal of prerecorded sound effects, a member of the technical staff can "play" the fight, adding the required sound as the action takes place onstage. Such a process removes knaps from the actor's responsibility and allows for a greater variety of sound than could be achieved in the theatre just a few years ago.

In addition, a vast array of other sound effects can be added to a theatrical fight. Crashes (from crash boxes), whistles, buzzers, slaps (generated by slap-sticks), bone-breaks, gunshots, and background music can all be easily added into a fight's orchestration, and like knapping these (and other) special sound effects may vary greatly in pitch, volume, quality, and duration. These sounds, like any element of a fight, must therefore be chosen carefully and blended into the overall orchestration so that the encounter is clarified, precise character statements are made, and the plot of the play is advanced.

Music in the Blades

In his book *Fight Directing for the Theatre,* J. Allen Suddeth refers to the rhythmic patterns of the cuts, parries, footwork, and vocal exchanges of the performers as the "music in the blades" (77–79). This music is another point to consider in the orchestration of a fight sequence. In one sense, however, Suddeth's definition is not fully descriptive, for the "music" to which he refers may be created by any objects used in a physical encounter, whether used for offensive or defensive purposes, and may include sounds produced by sticks, bottles, knives, chairs, etc. As with the other sound elements discussed, how these objects are used and the nature of the sound developed in their use (or in creating the illusion of their application) are critical factors in how they complement the physical dialogue and orchestration of the encounter.

Because anything is possible within a real fight, anything should be possible in a stage encounter. The music of the encounter, then, does not emanate solely from the weapons or props used (although that does affect the pitch and tone emitted); rather, it is the value of the action performed (with the prop or weapon) that determines the orchestration of the fight. Because every movement within a fight possesses a specific value or significance to the character executing it, its ultimate value is established by the motivation for the action, the objective of the action, the character's commitment to that action, and its relative worth or utility. Obviously, because not every action carries the same value for the character performing it, the resulting sounds will be perceived as different by an audience. A "false" or trick attack, for example, has a different value than a thrust intended to hit home. As a consequence, the false or trick attack will sound distinctly different from the thrust, despite the use of the same weapon.

Rhythm

Seldom do fights have a single steady beat where each action and re-action have the same regulated weight and speed. Rather fights are as varied and variable in tempo as the emotions that drive them. Conse-quently, stage fights should be fast at times, slow at others, sometimes predictable, sometimes sporadic and unpredictable. The rhythm and du-ration of the actions within the fight are first established by the emo-tions and the objectives of the characters and then carried out through their actions.

Orchestrating the Language of Violence

As mentioned earlier, the control of pitch, rhythm, duration, volume, and quality exercised by the sound effects technician and/or the foley artist in the sound design of a movie fight helps to shape the story of that fight. Although the theatre is not yet as sophisticated as the re-cording studio, high-quality sound design is essential to producing a good stage fight. This is true whether the piece is comic or dramatic, contemporary or classic. Regardless of the social class(es) of the fighters or the culture or period in which a physical encounter takes place, there are appropriate and specific sounds to their language of violence. Each fight is as unique as the characters involved, their circumstances, and their surroundings, and the artists involved must understand the world of the fight, "visit" that world, and then listen to the fight. It is im-perative that each encounter be orchestrated both visually and aurally to coordinate and support every aspect of the world of the play.

Whether these sounds are created in a studio or produced live on-stage, they effectively shape the audience's perception of the fight. To properly orchestrate the overall sound of the fight, all variables involved must complement, not compete with, one another. The sounds must be strategically mingled with one another to help the audience understand the characters, their motives, and the story of the fight, for that is the purpose, after all, of the language of violence. The orchestration of sound within a stage fight, therefore, should be done in such a way that if it were recorded on an audiocassette and played back or "observed" with the eyes closed, a listener could still understand the "language" of the encounter.

The need for proper orchestration of sound and silence in the presentation of fights on the dramatic stage must never be underestimated. There is certainly a basis of truth in the cliché that actions can, and do, speak louder than words; and the specific sounds of and around those actions are necessary to enhance and clarify them for the observer. Without the proper emphasis on the audible portion of a violent act, a valuable part of the story can be misunderstood or even lost. If violence is to remain a useful tool for the theatre artist, that artist must not only address the act itself—its image and effects—but the language of violence as well.

Works Cited

Girard, Dale Anthony. 1996. *Actors On Guard: A Practical Guide for the Use of the Rapier and Dagger for Stage and Screen.* New York: Theatre Arts Books, Routledge.

Hobbs, William. 1995. *Fight Direction for Stage and Screen.* London: A & C Black.

Martinez, Joseph. 1982. *Combat Mime: A Non-Violent Approach to Stage Violence.* Chicago: Nelson-Hall.

———. 1996. *The Swords of Shakespeare.* Jefferson, N.C.: McFarland.

Raphael, Bonnie. 1989. "The Sounds of Violence." *Fight Master* 10, no. 1:12–15; no. 2:8–13; no. 3:8–10.

Singleton, Ralph S. 1990. *Filmmaker's Dictionary.* Beverly Hills: Heinemann Press.

Suddeth, J. Allen. 1996. *Fight Directing for the Theatre.* Portsmouth, N.H.: Heinemann Press.

Figuring the Fight

Recovering Shakespeare's Theatrical Swordplay

Colleen Kelly

"THEY FIGHT." With these two words Shakespeare employs a vocabulary of very specific physical action to further plot and reveal character. Folio text, quartos, and modern editions of Shakespeare's plays present these words as stage directions isolated from the spoken text either by italics, columns in the margin, or enclosure in parentheses or brackets.[1] As a fight director I find this separation from the spoken text to be both challenging and disconcerting: challenging because the dramatic narrative becomes a singular physical event that must be configured—figured out—through choreographed swordplay, disconcerting because this marginalization is echoed in the common practice of isolating the fight from the process of textual inquiry. The examination of the fight for possible literary and dramatic through-lines, as well as the reverberations of those choices, is the first function of a fight director; translating those choices into a physical vocabulary of swordplay is the second. Because "they fight" is an element of the text, it must be examined with consideration to the textual whole and in collaboration with other interpreters.

Scholarship in Renaissance swordplay offers some insight into sword fighting in Elizabethan England. How *they* fought, however, does not

---

[1] All quotes are from The Arden Shakespeare. The stage direction "They fight" appears in *Romeo and Juliet* on five occasions. Scholars argue that Shakespeare may not have penned any of these directions. However, because these stage directions appear in extant Elizabethan play texts and are indicative of Elizabethan printing, as well as stage practice, for the purpose of this paper I treat all stage directions as though Shakespeare included them in his manuscripts.

explain what Shakespeare meant by "they fight." The functional use of swordplay, although reflective of character behavior, is different from the theatrical use of swordplay. A *theatrical* vocabulary of swordplay is required to create textual through-lines, and unfortunately, "they fight" is among the terms of Shakespeare's theatrical vocabulary whose meanings have yet to be recovered. The recovery process is difficult. As Alan Dessen suggests in *Recovering Shakespeare's Theatrical Vocabulary,* "[T]he most important reason for the difficulties in recovering Shakespeare's theatrical vocabulary is painfully simple. Most of the relevant evidence, including many things so obvious to players and playgoers in the 1590s and early 1600s as to be taken for granted, has been lost—as much as ninety percent, perhaps even more" (6). The process of recovery is further complicated by textual truisms and stage conventions that evolved in the absence of this vocabulary and that are currently accepted as historically accurate.

Scholarship in the methods of Elizabethan swordplay and current developments in methods of theatrical swordplay combine to provide a physical vocabulary that services modern productions. But what vocabulary did Shakespeare employ with "they fight," and how did his company of actors execute this stage direction? What did Elizabethan audiences see and how did they interpret the action? Aside from the text itself and speculation based on bits of scholarship imported from other fields, not much evidence exists with which to answer these questions. The complex nature of the recovery/discovery process is explained by Dessen: "To unravel these various threads requires a combination of skills (editor-textual critic, bibliographer, theatre historian, theatrical professional, historical scholar), but these figures, each expert in his or her own arena, do not speak the same languages. . . . To seek to recover a lost theatrical vocabulary is therefore to confront a language barrier that stands both between us and the age of Shakespeare and between groups of academic and theatrical interpreters today" (11). In this article I will probe this language barrier for the purpose of considering "they fight" as an essential element in the literary and dramatic composition of Shakespeare's text.

Shakespeare's use of the sword as text is evidence that Shakespeare, as well as his actors and his audience, understood not only swordplay's mechanics but also its complex intertext of behavior known as the *code duello* (rules governing the reasons for fighting and the manner in which duels were arranged). By the late 1500s swordplay was no longer a language exclusively owned by aristocrats. "By the reign of Elizabeth I, in peace as well as war, even the common man had access to swords, and it was well he did. . . . [T]his was, after all, still a time in which a man might involuntarily be 'pressed' into military service or challenged to a duel" (Turner and Soper xvii–xviii). Because knowing the language of the sword was not only common but necessary in Elizabethan society, it is reasonable to assume that Shakespeare and members of his company knew something of sword fighting. In fact, "at least one famous Elizabethan actor (Richard Tarleton) was known to be a 'London Master of Defence'—a title that required many years of formal training with the popular weapons of the day" (Martinez 1). Further, it is recounted in Holmes's *Elizabethan London* that Shakespeare, Kemp, and Burbage's two sons "with swords close at hand should the landlord appear . . . dismantled Burbage's Theatre for transport to the new site" (in Turner and Soper xix).

When Shakespeare appropriated the sword as a vehicle for dramatic narrative, the behavioral code of the *duello* could remain an intact signifier because its function in society and its function in theatre were one and the same. However, the functional technique of swordplay in society—to inflict or prevent bodily harm—was not synonymous with its function in the theatre. Even a swordsman such as Tarleton would be required to use his sword skill to serve the dramatic action of the play. Sword technique, therefore, needed to be reconfigured to serve a new purpose; swordplay for the stage needed to become its own unique theatrical language.

Turner and Soper decry the lack of scholarly interest in swordplay— behavioral, technical, functional, and theatrical—noting that "scholars of the Renaissance, who would not hesitate to further investigate almost any word, punctuation, or stage direction in Shakespeare, have been surprisingly mute about such open-ended notations as 'they fight' " (xiii–xiv). Although scholars have been especially disinclined to consider swordplay architecturally essential to the structure of the textual whole, I suggest textual inquiry in absence of "they fight" is an examination in absence of an essential textual element. Further, despite the fact that only scant and scattered bits of supportive evidence are available, I assert that for practical as well as textual reasons Shakespeare's fights must have been fully or at least partially choreographed. This assumption is based on the observation that his company members did not die as a result of sword fighting in the plays in which they performed. I also make this assumption because to repeat the play means to repeat the action of the fight. Romeo, for example, must come between Tybalt and Mercutio; Mercutio must be hurt under Romeo's arm ("Why the devil came you between us? I was hurt under your arm" [*Romeo and Juliet* 3.1.104–5]). It seems reasonable, then, that the actors performing these fights agreed to perform specific actions as the text required without injuring each other. Therefore, two imperatives that guide modern fight directors must also have applied to the staging of Shakespeare's fights: that they be dramatically effective and that they be safe.

Elizabethan audience members were "knowledgeable about quality swordplay" (Turner and Soper xx). They witnessed war and personal violence on the street, military spectacle in pageants, sportive competitions in tournaments, extravagant displays in masques, and the demonstration of advanced swordplay skill known as *playing the prize,* a recreation often held in theatres. It was a fashionable pastime to watch expert swordsmen test and prove their sword skill (Tarleton played his Master's Prize in 1587), and exposure to such a variety of functional and theatrical sword events created an audience capable of brutally judging a "staged" fight.

Occasionally, Shakespeare borrowed these militaristic and sportive vocabularies of function and entertainment, not necessarily using them in their fully realized form, but employing them as symbol and/or image. The masque is of special interest because evidence exists that the masques' combative ballets, mock battles, and sword dances were choreographed. These elaborate dance/fights were specifically figured for royal masques by dance choreographers "who were so highly regarded that they sometimes commanded more fees than either Inigo Jones the designer or Ben Jonson the writer" (Brissenden 17). Noting that the extravagances of court masques were beyond the normal resources of the average theatre company, Brissenden also points out that "the allegorical significance of heraldic devices could be, and was, used dramatically" (Brissenden 79).

Whereas dance and swordplay served a functional purpose in Elizabethan society, each served a theatrical purpose for Shakespeare and his contemporaries as well, offering dramatic characters codified physical languages through which to communicate, as well as intertexts of social signifiers dictating behavior.[2] Mark Franko, in *The Dancing Body in Renaissance Choreography,* defines the latter as the "conception of the dance as a political and civil virtue . . . a complex of rules for civil behavior directly marking civil demeanor as a systematic system for the dancing body, mediated by courtesy books" (11). As previously noted, this "complex of rules for civil behavior" in swordplay is known as the

---

[2]As evidenced in their content and reflected in titles such as *The Book of Honor and Armes* (Sir William Segar 1590) manuals in both dance and defense taught modes of behavior. Reciprocally, books of courtesy encouraged the mastery of dance and fence.

code duello. When Shakespeare used dance or swordplay as text, he not only endowed a character with a particular technical skill, he also gave that character a behavioral code against which he or she was measured by other characters and the audience. These codes conveyed both privilege and responsibility. Characters might, for example, have the freedom to flirt with a partner while dancing, or kill a neighbor when dishonored; but these same codes also imposed the *burden* of this behavior upon them.

Dance and swordplay are composed of separate and unique behavioral codes and physical techniques; however, they have social mores of virtue and honor and practical applications of science and mathematics in common. Both dance and defense manuals of the period, for example, cite shared movement principles such as space, distance, time, measure, and weight and present illustrated "figuring" of the individual's use of the body and the body in relationship to a partner.

Much scholarly emphasis has been focused on Shakespeare's use of the "figure" as it relates to speech, yet Shakespeare also used physical figures that are equally deserving of analysis. In fact, Shakespeare used recognizable dance configurations in "twelve plays certainly, fifteen probably" (Brissenden 16). In dance, the word *figure* is defined as a body—the human presence. It is also the posture and gesture the human figure creates. "Figure" is both pose and action. "Figure" is a sequence of movements the individual performs—patterns traced on the floor and shapes carved in space. Further, the relationship between two figures (bodies) creating figures (shapes and patterns) is also called a "figure"—a dance figure. And finally, when many figures (bodies) create dance figures (shapes and patterns in relationship) it is called a "figure"—a dance.

In *Much Ado about Nothing* (2.1), for example, figures of speech and figures of dance are intimately woven to create an aural and visual "figure" that emerges as a single and distinct impression.[3] This meshing of word and action to create a singular dramatic thought is, as contemporary playwright Suzan-Lori Parks suggests, a process of "figuring" (3–4). Such a process allows us (for the purpose of this article at least) to view the playwright as a "figurer" and ourselves, the artist-interpreters, as those who "figure out" the play.

Contained within the grand configuration of the text is the physical

---

[3]The stage directions "they step aside," as well as clues in the dialogue, indicate, according to Brissenden, that a pavan is an obvious choice for the first dance. See Brissenden 49–50 for a complete analysis.

figure of the fight. Fight figures are made manifest through the embodied physical action of swordplay just as poetic figures manifest themselves through speech, "not as patterns isolated from the rest, but as elements contributing to something larger, with the smaller and the larger primarily an expression of what the character feels and wants" (Joseph 5). When "what a character feels and wants" is moving toward "they fight," what emerges from the figuring process is the *character of the fight.*

Methods of discovering character are reviewed in a wealth of books giving instruction on the reading and performing of Shakespeare's text. In general, at least two principles about Shakespeare's language are agreed upon: first, at its core it is a visceral experience for both speaker and listener; second, its literary and dramatic aspects are interdependent. Linklater addresses the visceral in *Freeing Shakespeare's Voice:* "Shakespeare's text integrates words, emotions, objectives, intentions and actions, and in so doing it accurately reflects the Elizabethan society to whom it spoke. . . . Language lived in the body. Thought was experienced in the body. Emotions inhabited the organs of the body" (6). For the second principle—the interdependence of the literary and the dramatic—I turn to Joseph, "for on the one hand, the poetic quality of the lines can be fully realized only when they are spoken in character; yet, on the other, the completely imagined and truthful character can itself be realized only when the qualities of the literary text are taken into account at some stage of preparation" (xvii). Both of these authors acknowledge that it takes effort and practice to read, interpret, embody, perform, and listen to Shakespeare and that the Elizabethan understanding and use of language (especially poetic language) is foreign to contemporary interpreters—to borrow Shakespeare's own words: "they [Elizabethans] speak a language that I understand not" (*Winter's Tale* 3.2.79).

Ironically, to aid us in learning this language we "understand not," most authors invite us to (re)turn to the human body, to rely on our intimate understanding of breath and heartbeat and on our primordial memory of music and dance. Linklater companions a social response to the visceral experience of words: "If you have been doing these exercises with another person or several others, you will probably have found that sounds irresistibly cause interactions. Thus it is clear that even before logical meaning fires the engines of communication, communication of a fairly sophisticated nature can occur" (23). There is a primal experiential power in words that engages our senses and affects the audience, a power that Shakespeare, like playwright Thomas Dekker, used to dramatic advantage. Dekker "claimed that a good playwright could secure attention and admiration by the musical harmony of his writing, irrespective of what the audience understood of his meaning [and] could control an unruly audience by its own attraction" (in Brown 18–19).

This visceral dimension of Shakespeare's poetry is of special consideration when figuring "they fight." The human relationship to rhythm, as it relates to order and disorder, is the *heart* of personal and communal balance. Testing boundaries through the rhythms of sound and movement defines who characters are as individuals, their relationship with others, and their place in society and the universe. Brown suggests that experiencing Shakespeare's language "without concern for the meaning of words as parts of a whole . . . reveals the field of thought and sensation, the weight and muscularity of verbal expression" (16). William McNeill, in recalling his own personal response to military drilling in *Keeping Together in Time: Dance and Drill in Human History,* composed the phrase "muscular bonding" to describe the euphoric feeling and sense of boundary loss: "Obviously, something visceral was at work; something, I later concluded, far older than language and critically important in human history, because the emotion it arouses constitutes an indefinitely expansible basis for social cohesion among any and every group that keeps together in time, moving big muscles together and chanting, singing, or shouting rhythmically" (2).

The power of this rhythmic muscular bonding is at the core of ritual, religion, communal labor, politics, military combat, and personal combat. It invites trance, celebration, solidarity, ceremony, rebellion, and honor. It shapes and defines spiritual and universal understandings of balance and harmony and dictates personal and social boundaries of inclusion and exclusion. What is at the heart of this power? McNeill speculates that "rhythmic input from muscles and voice, after gradually suffusing through the entire nervous system, may provoke echoes of the fetal condition when major and perhaps principal external stimulus to the developing brain was the mother's heartbeat" (7).

Offering a means for an actor to discover Shakespeare's dramatic pulse—his poetry built on the iambic rhythm of the body—Linklater suggests: "Listen to your heartbeat when you've been exerting yourself, or listen to a baby's heartbeat—it goes . . . weak/strong, weak/strong, weak/strong" (122–23). Derivatives of the term *iambic* (as reviewed by Linklater) conjure images of life forces moving toward objectives: "drive forth, to assail, to shoot . . . push, persistency, determination, aspiration . . . steady thrust forward" (123). Thus, textual iambic rhythm is a visceral element that often reveals, through regular or irregular patterning, a character's physical state and the physical state toward which that character is moving.

We also derive understanding of characters from the sounds of the words they utter. Obviously, the poetic language and imagery in the dialogue provide significant clues to the physical state that a particular character is in and whether that state is governed by emotion or reason. Identifying physical states is important because a character must be in a specific physical state in order to execute specific physical action such as "they fight." In addition, other characters recognize and engage in those states and the audience, hopefully (or helplessly as Dekker asserts), recognizes and engages in those states.

In the first scene of *Romeo and Juliet,* for example, Gregory and Sampson engage in wordplay about the physical state necessary for "they fight":

SAMPSON: I strike quickly being moved.
GREGORY: But thou are not quickly moved to strike.
SAMPSON: A dog of the house of Montague moves me.
GREGORY: To move is to stir, and to be valiant is to stand;
Therefore, if thou art moved, thou runn'st away.
SAMPSON: A dog of that house shall move me to stand.
I will take the wall of any man or maid of Montague's. (1.1.5–11)

In debating whether they really have the courage to *take up* their masters' quarrel, they refer to the physical state a person must be in to *take* such action, in this instance, to be moved to fight. Not long after, Romeo describes his inability to be moved toward the physical state needed to dance at the Capulet ball:

ROMEO: Give me a torch, I am not for this ambling.
Being but heavy I will bear the light.
MERCUTIO: Nay, gentle Romeo, we must have you dance.
ROMEO: Not I, believe me. You have dancing shoes
with nimble soles, I have a soul of lead
So stakes me to the ground I cannot move. (1.4.11–22)

Smitten by unrequited love that burdens him, Romeo cannot find the *lightness of being* required of a dancer and therefore is unprepared to participate; he cannot *rise to the occasion.*

Later in the play, when he is newly filled with love for Juliet, Romeo's physical state is challenged again. This time he is invited to fight, and again he is unable (or unwilling) to be moved. Tybalt, through poetic meter, attacks Romeo with a strong beat and then clearly offers a repetitive weak/strong rhythm as a challenge:

TYBALT: Romeo, the love I bear thee can afford
no better term than this: thou art a villain. (3.1.59–60)

Tybalt has rhythmically given the challenge to Romeo. Tybalt is waiting, the other characters onstage are waiting, and the audience is waiting. In response Romeo begins to take up the challenge, echoing the rhythmic pattern that was given him by Tybalt and momentarily moving Tybalt, the other observing characters, and the audience closer to a potential "they fight." Then he changes. Romeo does not give the challenge (the 'villain') back again. Instead, he reverses the stress pattern of the poetic rhythm on "doth much excuse" and moves the scene in the opposite direction.[4] There will be no fight, not now:

> ROMEO: Tybalt, the reason that I have to love thee
> Doth much excuse the appertaining rage
> To such a greeting: villain am I none,
> Therefore farewell. I see thou knowest me not. (3.1.61–64)

Later in the scene Romeo again reverses direction, this time to match the passion of "the furious Tybalt." Now it's time to fight. Now the give and take of the earlier challenge will culminate. Needing to avenge Mercutio's death, Romeo conjures the physical state that such action will require:

> ROMEO: Again, in triumph, and Mercutio slain.
> Away to heaven respective lenity,
> And fire-ey'd fury be my conduct now!
> Now, Tybalt, take the 'villain' back again. (3.1.124–27)

Romeo's shift to the physical state of fury, is figured in the rhythm of the lines as well as the words themselves.[5] The gathering of strength from a series of equal strong beats, noted by Linklater to have been used for religious expression, is reminiscent of McNeill's description of the strong, repetitive structure of martial drilling used to invoke power

---

[4]Psychological analysis of Romeo's situation may produce some interesting character choices, but essentially Romeo doesn't fight because the poetic structure doesn't move him in that direction. Whether governed by emotion, reason, or a combination of the two, Romeo's present state does not accommodate violence, and it is configured in one of the following patterns: (**LOVE** thee) **DOTH** much **EX CUSE**; (**LOVE** thee) **DOTH** much ex **CUSE**; (**LOVE** thee) **DOTH MUCH** ex **CUSE**; (**LOVE** thee) doth **MUCH** ex **CUSE**. Each configuration reveals a different character choice, such as gracefully bows out, chickens-out, abruptly backs down, confuses the issue, backpedals, gets tripped up, is tongue-tied, diffuses the situation, embraces Tybalt, forces Tybalt to be taken aback, throws Tybalt off guard, patronizes Tybalt, mocks Tybalt.

[5]In *Antony and Cleopatra* Enobarbus defines this physical state of being furious: "Now he'll outstare the lightning. To be furious is to be frighted out of fear, and in that mood the dove will peck the estridge" (3.13.200–202).

through muscular activity (125). Also of import in figuring the physical action moving toward "they fight" is the repetition of the word *now*, noted by Joseph as a figure in speech (epizeuxis) in which a word is repeated with vehemence or some other distinguishing emphasis (196). A few lines later, on "this shall determine that," the text offers the possibility for Romeo to overtake Tybalt with a *sprung rhythm*, which Linklater describes as a rhythm having "more immediate physicality to it. . . . [A] sprung rhythm means that a weak stress springs up to meet the stronger stress on its own level or even to subdue it" (125).

Examining the poetic and literary elements of the text for the action of the fight, however, is only part of the equation. The language of the sword has its own voice and gesture. Elements such as space, time, weight, and sound must be configured with the elements of the poetic and literary languages. The physical relationship between Tybalt and Romeo is now determined by the length of a sword.

How is this relationship established and how is it violated? The earlier conflict between Romeo and Tybalt was unresolved. Romeo did not give the 'villain' back again; he was not moved to fight. What will Romeo do now? Similar to the search for the shape of a dance figure, I look at the concrete nature of the text for floor patterns and spatial shapes:

> BENVOLIO: **Here comes** the furious Tybalt **back again.**
> ROMEO: **Again,** in triumph, and Mercutio slain.
> **Away** to heaven respective lenity,
> And fire-ey'd fury be my conduct **now!**
> **Now,** Tybalt, take the 'villain' **back again**
> That late thou gav'st me, for Mercutio's soul
> Is but a little way above our heads,
> **Staying** for thine to keep him company.
> Either thou, or I, or both must **go** with him.
> TYBALT: Thou wretched boy, that didst consort him **here,**
> Shalt with him **hence.**
> ROMEO: This shall determine that. *They fight. Tybalt falls.* (3.1.123–33)

What is the first sound or gesture from the language of the sword that we see or hear? Tybalt entering with his sword already drawn? The sound of a sword (or swords) drawing? The contact of swords? No sword sounds at all? Ask a child to draw an imaginary sword and you will hear: "*sh-sh-sh-shwiii-t.*" Within lines 132–33 are sounds such as: "did**st**," "con**sort**," "**shalt**," "**hence**," "**This**," "**shall**." These sounds can be part of a build that climaxes with the sounds of the swords themselves; or the sounds can be integrated with the sounds of the swords in action; or perhaps they are phantoms of sounds we never hear.

What is the time frame in which the action takes place? The earliest moment for Romeo to kill Tybalt would be on Tybalt's last word, *hence* (which just happens to lend itself to an expiration of breath). To accomplish this Romeo would need to rob Tybalt of his last poetic beat, overcoming him with the word *this* and the physical gesture of a thrust. Other choices include completing the metric foot between *hence* and *This* with drawing swords or engaging in exchanges; or delaying any swordplay until after Romeo finishes his last line to Tybalt (*This* then refers to the fight rather than the deathblow).

Dialogue and stage directions identify and clarify physical action and the *manner* in which action might be executed. When Benvolio is asked to recount the confrontation between Romeo and Tybalt he reports: "And to't they go like lightning" (3.1.174). To Benvolio *lightning* may mean fast or sudden, or it could mean Romeo and Tybalt executed glancing sword cuts that caused sparks to fly. Benvolio continues, "for, ere I / could draw to part them, was stout Tybalt slain, / And as he fell did Romeo turn and fly" (3.1.174–76). Although these lines may clarify the manner in which Romeo and Tybalt fought, they seemingly could contradict the manner in which Romeo left the scene.

> BENVOLIO: Romeo, away, be gone,
> The citizens are up, and Tybalt slain!
> Stand not amaz'd. The Prince will doom thee death
> If thou art taken. Hence, be gone, away!
> ROMEO: O, I am fortune's fool.
> BENVOLIO: Why dost thou stay?
> *Exit Romeo.* (3.1.134–138)

One possible solution to this apparent conflict in word and action is that Benvolio *lies* to protect himself and/or Romeo. As a fight director searching for the physical action of the fight, I would be remiss not to ask whether both can be true. Can Romeo "stay" *and* "fly"? Some possible answers can be found by examining the order in which actions might take place, the proximity of Romeo to Tybalt at the moment of the deathblow, and the time it might take for Tybalt to execute the stage direction that follows "they fight," which is "Tybalt falls."

Actions such as Romeo's sword entering Tybalt's body, the removal of the sword (if it is removed), Tybalt's response to the deathblow, his expiration and fall (or fall and expiration) can all be configured in ways that allow Romeo to stay and *then* fly as Tybalt falls. Romeo's staying to make sure Tybalt is dead and flying when he is assured Mercutio's death has been avenged ("Mercutio's soul is but a little way above our heads, *staying* for thine to keep him company) is one solution. The physical action of Tybalt falling between "Why dost thou stay?" and the stage direction "Exit Romeo" allows Benvolio's question to have an answer. Another choice is for Tybalt's falling body to force Romeo into his exit, thereby being banished from the stage by Tybalt himself. Numerous performance choices and scholarly interpretations are certainly possible. It is imperative, however, that all textual elements be considered.

The practice of finding accord between word and physical action in figures of speech is certainly nothing more than the practice of rhetoric, but when the text includes swordplay, *another language* has been added to the equation. With only two words, *they fight,* Shakespeare signifies the use of a complex language of theatrical swordplay. When configuring a fight, the fight director is searching the text for two languages: the language of rhetoric and the language of the sword. As Peter Brook notes, not only did Shakespeare possess a vocabulary of over twenty-five thousand words, but "in the theatre, there are infinitely more languages, beyond words, through which communication is established and maintained with the audience. There is body language, sound language, rhythm language, color language, costume language, scenery language, lighting language—all to be added to those 25,000 available words. Every element of life is like a word in a universal vocabulary" (113). "They fight" is therefore an element of the text denoting a figure of physical action composed of a theatrical vocabulary of violence. The process of discovering and configuring "they fight" is the process of discovering and configuring one vocabulary in relationship with many others. Such configuring reveals not merely a uni(t)fied but a unified text, one that, in keeping with Elizabethan sensibility, is a complete thought, a harmonious composition of elements.

Works Cited

Brissenden, Alan. 1981. *Shakespeare and the Dance.* New Jersey: Humanities Press.

Brook, Peter. 1993. *The Open Door: Thoughts on Acting and Theatre.* New York: Pantheon.

Brown, John Russell. 1970. *Shakespeare's Dramatic Style.* London: Heinemann Educational Books.

Dessen, Alan C. 1995. *Recovering Shakespeare's Theatrical Vocabulary.* Cambridge: Cambridge University Press.

Franko, Mark. 1986. *The Dancing Body in Renaissance Choreography (c. 1416–1589).* Birmingham, Ala.: Summa Publications.

Hobbs, William. 1995. *Fight Direction for Stage and Screen.* London: A & C Black.

Joseph, Bertram. 1981. *Acting Shakespeare*. New York: Theatre Arts Books.

Linklater, Kristin. 1992. *Freeing Shakespeare's Voice: The Actor's Guide to Talking the Text*. New York: Theatre Communications Group.

Martinez, J. D. 1996. *The Swords of Shakespeare: An Illustrated Guide to Stage Combat Choreography in the Plays of Shakespeare*. Jefferson, N.C.: McFarland.

McNeill, William H. 1995. *Keeping Together in Time: Dance and Drill in Human History*. Massachusetts: Harvard University Press.

Parks, Suzan-Lori. 1995. "Possession." *The America Play and Other Works*. New York: Theatre Communications Group.

Shakespeare, William. 1986. *The Arden Edition of the Works of William Shakespeare*. Ed. Richard Proudfoot. New York: Methuen.

Turner, Craig, and Tony Soper. 1990. *Methods and Practice of Elizabethan Swordplay*. Carbondale, Ill.: Southern Illinois University Press.

Postmodern Violence and

Human Solidarity:

Sex and Forks in *Shopping and Fucking*

Leslie A. Wade

MARK RAVENHILL'S *SHOPPING AND FUCKING*, which enjoyed a highly successful run during the summer of 1997 in London's West End and recently opened Off Broadway in New York, has intrigued theatregoers on both sides of the Atlantic because of its graphic treatment of urban violence and merchandised sex. One critic recommended the play for only "the strong of stomach" (Taylor 7). Ravenhill's work revels in its shocking effects and sexual simulations. Indeed, the most remarked-upon sequence in the play, in which the central character (Mark) reams a young prostitute and rises up with blood on his mouth, may take its place alongside the baby-stoning scene in Edward Bond's *Saved* as one of the most grisly dramatic enactments in recent British theatre history.

Beyond its sensationalist aspect, however, *Shopping and Fucking* poses for its audience some very basic questions concerning the contemporary moment and its disconnections. It is my contention that the play well dramatizes the confusions, impasses, and emotional vertigo of the postmodern condition and that the depiction of violence is an attending consequence. And, its guttersnipe sensibility notwithstanding, I view Ravenhill's work as ultimately ethical in its focus and philosophical in its resolution, with a conclusion that begs reflection regarding personal freedom, identity, interdependence, and the viability of human solidarity.

Ravenhill's play chronicles the travails of Mark, Lulu, and Robbie, three alienated young Londoners who have bonded to form a surrogate family. When Mark enters a detox program, his two housemates turn to drug dealing for income, a move that involves them with a drug-trafficking producer who is both a sadist and a high-art aficionado. Mark returns from rehab, having renounced his chemical and emotional dependencies, and determines to have no sex but impersonal sex. The decision propels him into league with Gary, a teenage prostitute, with whom Mark ultimately falls in love. Marching through sundry depictions of abuse, exploitation, and violence, the play culminates in a moral conundrum for Mark that provokes mixed responses in the viewer. Should he take the fork and wield it upon Gary as an erotic weapon? In plainest terms, should he stick the fork up Gary's ass? And what does all this have to do with human solidarity?

In the opening sequence of *Shopping and Fucking* Lulu stands over Mark, who is suffering heroin withdrawal, and maternally spoon-feeds him from a take-out tin. Mark swallows, then summarily vomits, providing the audience with a repulsive visceral image that works to highlight the dysfunctional aspect of this quasi-familial confederation. In repeated instances Ravenhill depicts the failure of social bonding and communal interactions. Lulu sees her biological family only on the rare holiday; Gary is terrorized by his abusive stepfather; Brian mutilates his clients who fail to pay their debts in a timely fashion. It is indeed this communal dissociation that is underscored when Lulu tells of witnessing the slashing of a convenience-store clerk. She confesses to feeling no impulse to intervene; she, in fact, walks out of the store with a pilfered candy bar.

Ravenhill's play is quite compelling in its portrayal of the many breakdowns of contemporary capitalist culture, and the work's sensibility is decidedly postmodern. Media images and technologies are pervasive. Brian, the ruthless drug boss, is enamored of Disney's *The Lion King*. Videotapes are used in numerous instances. Robbie and Lulu operate a phone-sex line to pay off their drug debt. The virtual realities of the play are highlighted by Gary's apartment, located on the second floor above a video arcade. The screen and the lure of its surface orient and determine behaviors, as in the shopping scene, when Gary performs oral sex on Mark before the gaze of the store's surveillance camera. Such postmodern earmarks, of course, suggest the evacuation of foundational depth. Fractured realities and multiple perspectives have become matter-of-fact. In this play even Robbie, who cannot hold a job in a fast-food restaurant, can expound on the culture's loss of its master narratives: "I think a long time ago there were big stories. Stories so big you could live your whole life in them. The Powerful Hands of the Gods and Fate. The Journey to Enlightenment. The March of Socialism. But they all died or the world grew senile or forgot them, so now we're making up our own stories. Little stories" (Ravenhill 63).

Postmodern thought has set itself in opposition to the tradition of humanism and its teleological assurances. Postmodernism has served to expose and undermine categories of subjectivity based on appeals to reason, objectivity, universality, and the abstracted ego. One recalls Lyotard's appeal for the "inhuman," a condition of indeterminacy unbounded by humanist constraints.[1] Ravenhill's play, I believe, effectively explores the complexion and parameters of postmodern relations. His characters exist in a space where categories have crumbled, where affiliations have undergone extreme realignment. Each character undertakes his or her own self-fashioning narrative and enters a realm of the polymorphous libido.

On a basic level the postmodern equates to the posthuman, and in the recent text *Posthuman Bodies* Judith Halberstam and Ira Livingston welcome the collapse of human categories and configurations. According to this outlook, the posthuman marks a new state of liberation and potentiality and embraces the wholesale razing of conventional communal associations. Halberstam and Livingston continue: "The human tribe can never again be family. Postfamilial bodies celebrate the end of His-and-Her matching theories that endlessly revolve around the miserable imagined unit, the imagined community of an imagined kinship in an imagined house" (10).

In Timberlake Wertenbaker's recent play, *Three Birds Alighting on a Field,* the character Stephen, an independent-minded painter, declares that moral issues have gone out of fashion but might return—for six months or so, he opines. Despite the obscenity, violence, and affrontive elements depicted in *Shopping and Fucking,* the play is, at its core, a play about ethics (albeit posthuman ethics) that grapples with the issues of kinship and connection in the face of a dehumanizing social and economic order.

I would underscore three different ethical postures presented in the play, each representing different conceptions of human interconnection

---

[1]This feature of Lyotard's work is concisely explained by Sim (119–37). In my use of the term *posthuman,* I am speaking of the loss of those traits that have traditionally been ascribed to humanity and have served to privilege humankind as an elevated life-form endowed with reason, aspiration, spirituality, etc. According to poststructuralist thought, there is no essential quality that defines the human. As a category "humanity" is thus malleable and open to reinvention. The posthuman outlook is premised on this assumption and looks toward a future in which bodies and selves are not fixed but fluid.

and moral obligation. Ironically, it is the brutish TV producer, Brian, who serves as the mouthpiece for humanism in the traditional sense. He shows videos of his son playing the cello and remarks on the benefits of high art—on how beauty elevates. Later Brian declaims on the need for order, for purpose, for clarity: "We need something. A guide. A talisman. A set of rules. A compass to steer us through this everlasting night" (84). The persuasive aspect of Brian's rhetoric, in fact, prompted one critic to comment: "It's typical of this intense, unsettling play that the most truthful (and very nearly the only coherent) thoughts are expressed by the character who's a stand-in for Satan" (Zoglin 95). However, we later come to learn that this sociopathic TV producer upholds humanist values in large part because they support the economic food chain and endorse a vertical order of having and not having. In this scheme prescribed values regulate the flow of capital and the inclusion/ exclusion of variant human bodies.

A contrasting ethical outlook is evidenced midway through the piece, when Robbie delivers an oddly affecting speech recounting a drug experience and its attendant vision of human interconnection: "Listen this is the important bit. If you'd felt . . . I felt. I was looking down on this planet. Spaceman over this earth. And I see this kid in Rwanda, crying but he doesn't know why. And this granny in Kiev, selling everything she's ever owned. And this president in Bogota or . . . South America. And I see the suffering. And the wars. And the grab, grab, grab. And I think: Fuck Money. Fuck it. This selling. This buying. This system. Fuck the bitching world and let's be . . . beautiful. Beautiful. And happy. You see? You see?" (37).

In this passage we note a movement toward the universal and all-inclusive. However, this image is presented as somewhat facile and nostalgic and produces a comic effect. The vision's high-mindedness is made even more ironic by its status as a hallucination and by the fact that Robbie later proves himself eminently mean and egocentric. Ravenhill is not predisposed to any grand conception of human connectedness or global altruism. For the writer such an outlook seems outdated and too closely aligned with traditional moral thinking.

An alternative understanding of human connection and communal responsibility, however, arises in a third ethical posturing of the play, the one I believe advocated by the playwright himself; that is, the commitment to a radical freedom and the imperative to self-create. The characters in this piece act under no moral compulsion or social obligation. They are indifferent to legal, moral, or religious codes. For Ravenhill the communal order has no legitimate basis but coheres according to the logic of the marketplace. No master narrative serves to enliven or organize the world of these characters, so it is incumbent on each to self-fashion, to reject dependencies of various forms, and to assume a validity that is self-proclaimed.

It is curious that the fork functions as a dominant prop and symbol in Ravenhill's play. On the one hand, it represents the progress of civilization, the refinement of the barbaric, and all the codes that organize social intercourse around the table—the long-lived emblem of human communion. In this light the fork can be seen as the repository of cultural values, a testament to the ongoing process of humanizing. In *Shopping and Fucking,* however, the fork also takes on a malevolent aspect. Early in the play Robbie tells of his workday at a fast-food restaurant and his being attacked by an angry patron with a plastic fork. And at the climax of the piece, it is a fork that is foregrounded, when Mark crosses to impale Gary.

In the highly charged, climactic scene of *Shopping and Fucking,* Robbie and Lulu stage a play sequence in which Gary acts out his masochistic fantasies. The three imagine a disco setting and improvise a scenario in which Gary is picked up by a powerful protector who seizes and sexually savages him. As the play sequence escalates Robbie steps into the role of the dominator and initiates onstage a furious act of anal sex. Mark, who has up to this point refrained from the game playing, steps forward and abuses Gary in a similar fashion. It is then that Gary turns and asks for someone to be the "father" who will take something sharp and lethal and penetrate him again. Lulu and Robbie remonstrate. Mark, however, takes up a fork and accompanies Gary outside, leading the audience to understand that he will assist Gary in his demand, that he will extinguish the youth's emotional torment.

Ravenhill follows this sequence with a philosophical passage that attempts (although not quite successfully, I would argue) to justify Mark's decision. Mark relates a parable (a tale of science fiction) about a time centuries in the future when the "Earth has died" (87). Humanity (or, more precisely, posthumanity) has moved onto a satellite populated by mutants of multiple shape and hue. In this story Mark encounters an "ape thing" selling a beautiful slave, a well-tanned blonde endowed with a "three-foot dick." He buys the slave, then offers him his freedom. The slave, however, breaks down and begs to remain in his subjugated station. He despairs that he cannot feed himself or think for himself. The slave implores, "I'll be dead in a week." Mark responds, "That is a risk I'm prepared to take" (88). In this line Mark voices his preference for self-sufficiency over co-dependence, even if death is the consequence.

It is here that Ravenhill sets forth the basic ethic of the piece, one that valorizes freedom, rejects external social or moral claims, and esteems self-actualization above all else.

The attention *Shopping and Fucking* has received stems not simply from the play's sensationalism but also from its moral outlook, which is at times muddled and convoluted. In many respects it is a messy play, one that nevertheless can provoke, if not exasperate. To its credit the work addresses in its peculiar way the problematic ethics of the posthuman future. It also locates the source of violence. Violence issues in one form from the status quo hierarchy of capitalism and its supportive moral/aesthetic value system. This is a violence born of greed and coercion. Another form of violence stems from the postmodern modalities of alienation and virtuality that engender a flat affect, which recognizes no connection with the other.

What emerges from the play is a fundamental question of connectedness. Mark tells of laboring under numerous co-dependencies, and the play seeks to dramatize his overcoming of these dependencies and his move to a state of autonomy. *Shopping and Fucking* proclaims a radical freedom, and the posthuman world teases with the possibility of such freedom. But with radical freedom come numerous terrors, especially that of radical loneliness.

The aspect and trajectory of the posthuman order are pressing concerns for many artists and theorists. Certainly there is no consensus on the delineation of this realm or prescription for its direction. In her book *Presence and Desire* Jill Dolan recounts a piece of fiction by Pat Califia that details an experience in an s/m club where a person is put in a body bag and beaten by masked figures (185). Such an image prompts consideration of the body freed from identity claims or humanizing categories. Julia Kristeva, in her recent work, *Nations without Nationalism,* posits an alternative scenario. She looks to the future and calls for a "transnational principle of Humanity . . . a continuation of the stoic and Augustinian legacy . . . that we must henceforth go back to and bring up to date" (27).

Shopping and Fucking is a strident play that activates thinking about such questions. Its moral positioning is at times unfocused and contradictory. Even with Mark's assertion of radical freedom, his "forking" of Gary can be read as an act of ironic altruism. In that moment Mark signals his renunciation of civil behavior, yet he is affected by Gary's plea and seeks to alleviate the youth's emotional suffering. And at the play's conclusion the three who open the play are once again depicted together in tableau, alternately feeding one another: a restored, alternative family unit. Despite its inconsistencies and shortcomings, the play chafes and stirs largely, I believe, because of the powerful questions it summons. How is community possible for the posthuman order? How can we conceive of and realize a new-world solidarity—that is, a solidarity of strangers?[2]

Works Cited

Dean, Jodi. 1996. *Solidarity of Strangers: Feminism after Identity Politics.* Berkeley: University of California Press.

Dolan, Jill. 1993. *Presence and Desire.* Ann Arbor: University of Michigan Press.

Halberstam, Judith, and Ira Livingston. 1995. *Posthuman Bodies.* Bloomington: Indiana University Press.

Kristeva, Julia. 1993. *Nations without Nationalism.* New York: Columbia University Press.

Ravenhill, Mark. 1997. *Shopping and Fucking.* London: Methuen Drama.

Sim, Stuart. 1996. *Jean-François Lyotard.* New York: Prentice-Hall.

Taylor, Paul. 1996. "Theatre: Shopping and Fucking." *Independent,* 3 October, p. 7.

Zoglin, Richard. 1998. "Assault Play." *Time,* 16 February, p. 95.

---

[2]This question is investigated by Jodi Dean in *Solidarity of Strangers: Feminism after Identity Politics.*

Spanked to the Fringe

Lesbian Sadomasochism

Jane Barnette

L ESBIAN SADOMASOCHISM, the "extreme fringe of acceptable sexuality," has provoked much debate for second-wave lesbian feminists (Weeks 236–37). British sexuality scholar Jeffrey Weeks called sadomasochism the "theatre of sex," and it is in this light that I will examine lesbian s/m. This performative analysis is aware of both sides of the performance theory "double mirror" that Richard Schechner delineated in 1985: "There are two main realms of performance theory: (1) looking at human behavior—individual and social—as a genre of performance; (2) looking at performances—of theatre, dance, and other 'art forms'—as a kind of personal or social interaction" (296).[1]

The principal performance "text" that I will use in my analysis is an interview with a Northwestern University senior who was active in the lesbian s/m community in the mid-1990s, interspersed with narratives pulled from the San Francisco lesbian s/m organization Samois. By touching on both the dramatic and the political sides of s/m, I intend to expand on what Susan Farr explained in Samois's *Coming to Power:* "These two expressions, the playful and the powerful, come concretely together each time one of us feels the need to administer or submit to a spanking" (185).

Many young straight feminists first accepted lesbianism as a legitimate

---

[1] I am aware that Schechner derives this theory from others, drawing most notably from the fields of anthropology and psychoanalysis. I also recognize that his presence in this article about the feminist, transformative possibilities of lesbian s/m performance may seem incongruous, but I find his explanations most helpful in my analysis of (s/m) sex as a performative, even theatrical, event.

concern through reading Adrienne Rich's groundbreaking "Compulsory Heterosexuality and Lesbian Existence." As a result of Rich's "vanilla" (non-s/m) stance, the concept of lesbians—especially political and/or feminist lesbians—who engaged in s/m was unthinkable. Lesbianism was supposed to be a way of *resisting* heterosexism, of discover-[ing] the erotic in female terms," not simply another forum for exploiting power differentials (Rich 130). Hence Tacie Dejanikus's frustration when saying "the point [of feminism] is to get rid of power roles as much as possible" (25).

Whether or not the "point" of feminism (or indeed "the erotic in female terms") can be determined, some feminists believe that patriarchal power can be eradicated through the censorship of pornography. The slogan of the antipornography feminists is "Pornography is the theory, Rape is the practice," a saying coined by Robin Morgan (Weeks 233) to encapsulate the belief that pornography represents and even encourages an extreme patriarchal view of women, one that is most often also violent. More than any issue except abortion, pornography has bonded contemporary women together in a fight that is, to many, a fight for their lives.

The antiporn feminists have fueled the fire against lesbian s/m. Antiporn lesbian feminists find the portrayal of s/m in lesbian pornography disturbing because it places lesbians in the same category as those heterosexual women who were blinded by compulsory heterosexuality or, worse yet, in the ranks of phallic violence against women. In an article that started a volley of antiporn and pro-s/m writings, Andrea Zawinski transcribes the words of Dawn Lobell and Renee Mittler, cofacilitators of a workshop on lesbians and pornography. Zawinski quotes Lobell: "When you look at *White Women* by Helmet Newton . . . one woman is always dominant and the other submissive. They're portrayed as violent. It tells lies about lesbians like lesbians are the ones who rape" (9). By equating consensual s/m with violence, Pat Califia argues that this view is marked by "a typical degree of ignorance about s/m" (1980, 25). Califia was responding to the aforementioned article because Lobell and Mittler later identify her as "one of the leaders" of the lesbian s/m community. Califia is clear in her argument that "S/M is not violence" and "S/M is not 'conforming to sex roles' " (1980, 25).

Other pro-s/m lesbians make an explicit distinction between emotional s/m and sexual s/m, as one Samois member did under the pseudonym Juicy Lucy. Lucy talked about a "pattern of emotional pain" in lesbian relationships that she started calling "emotional S/M" (32). This negative, emotional s/m is quite different from the sexual s/m, which is, to Lucy, "very cathartic & healing for me" (35). Because of this release or catharsis, Lucy says, "a lot of nonspecific anxiety is gone from my life, especially anxiety around sex" (35). In this light sadomasochism between lesbians seems to be almost a cure for the ills of power differentials. Instead of reinforcing the oppressive nature of power, s/m subverts it by taking control of the power and allowing the partners to "own it" for themselves. The power of subversion is not a new theory, of course, and has also been applied to women's performance art. As Jeanie Forte says, "In defining the rules of the game [in feminist performance], a woman may take unprecedented control of her own image" (263).

In this way s/m can be seen as rebel sex, fighting the "real, painful violence against women [that] is being perpetrated all the time" (Califia 1980, 25). Moreover, because sexual s/m for lesbians seems always to involve planning, or at least understanding, the upcoming scene, "trust is an absolute essential" (Lucy 36). Usually s/m lesbians pick a "safe word" other than "no" or "stop" to signal the end of a scene. With this kind of control one could argue that sadomasochism is more egalitarian than "vanilla" sex. With a safe word as one's armor, one can escape the problem of "no really means yes" that may or may not be true in a sexual act, and reserve "mercy" or even "blue" for times of real pain and/or fear.

As even the language of "scene," "toys," "roles," etc. suggests, lesbian s/m can easily be viewed as performance.[2] "The roles in S/M sex," Califia argues, "should be compared to the roles adopted by actors during a play" (1980, 25). Here s/m explicitly becomes the "human behavior—individual and social—as a genre of performance" of which Schechner writes (295). In the same way that actors are encouraged "to act in-between identities," so too s/m players occupy this interstitial position. As "performing is a paradigm of liminality," I would argue that s/m is a rite of passage, a liminal performance, as well (Schechner 295). Through my interview text the idea of lesbian s/m as an interstitial rite of passage will become evident, as will the ideal of s/m as the "theatre of sex" that Weeks mentioned.

The ritual of s/m, according to my interviewee, Erica (all names are

---

[2]For most theatre scholars the theatre experience is incomplete without an audience. As Peter Brook has said, "in the theatre the audience completes the steps of production" (Brockett 8). Although I concede the need for an onlooker to distinguish theatre from ritual, I see the line between spectator and participant as flexible, sometimes nonexistent. In the private sexual activity I examine here as theatre, the audience consists both of the participants themselves and the absent, disapproving symbolic order that s/m confronts and challenges.

pseudonyms), begins with the planning. In her case, speaking of her first ever "scene," she was the "bottom" (masochist) to two "tops" (sadists). Enacting a scene with a ratio of two tops to one bottom is rare, for "most S/M people prefer the submissive 'bottom' or masochistic role" (Califia 1979, 19). Hence, most of the planning took place between the two tops, although "I told them what I didn't want done to me, and picked out toys I didn't want used," said Erica. Within the boundaries set by the masochist, the sadists then wrote the script of the evening, beginning with another ritual: a cocktail party. To "heighten" the rite, the two tops, Alexandra and Vicky, set the date for Erica's initiation to correspond with Alexandra's twenty-first birthday. At the party Erica's role as slave began, as she served all of the drinks and lit Alexandra's cigarettes on command. This interaction should not be confused with arguing that s/m roles become part of daily interaction, however, for as Erica stressed, "I *wanted* to be the little slave of the party. I asked them if I could do that."

When the foreplay of the party was over and the guests left, the actual s/m scene began. Symbolically refused the mask of clothing, Erica was told "not to bother putting her clothes back on." Naked against Alexandra's and Vicky's black mini-dresses and tights, Erica was told to lie down on the floor. In what Erica described as a "ritualistic" fashion, Alexandra and Vicky brought out two razors and little cereal bowls full of water. They then shaved Erica's wrists to prevent her from having her wrist hair torn off by the electrical tape they used to restrain her.

Hence, the beginning of the ritual was a bizarre combination of freedom and restraint, in the manner of what could be described as Schechner's "not-not not" quality.[3] The sadists were not freeing Erica but were not totally restraining her, yet they were not not doing those things either. Moreover, in the actual midst of the scene during which she was spanked with a mitt spiked with gold tacks, Erica described it as "hurting more, because I felt spikes going in my butt. It felt cool, though." So even the feelings caused *by* s/m occupy this threshold of "not-not not." Even the prelude to the ritual might be viewed from the perspective of not-not not, for as Erica described her feelings prior to the be-

---

[3]Schechner defines this "not-not not" trait within the context of his definition of performance as "restored behavior." The triple negative of not-not not attempts to explain the interstitial position of the performer who, when enacting a role, is not the character and yet not not the character either. In this state (akin to Lacan's *jouissance,* perhaps), the notions of Self and Other are blurred, and as Schechner remarks, it is "in this sense [that] performing is a paradigm of liminality" (123).

ginning of the entire scene, "I just sat in the living room by myself
going, 'what the fuck am I doing?' But being really excited nonetheless." In this moment Erica experienced what Califia calls the "edge of
pain, the edge that melts over and turns into pleasure," calling into
question what pleasure and pain really are and how related they are
(1979, 21).

Perhaps if one sees pleasure and pain as points on a continuum, Erica's
position as not-not not is then illustrative of the "full emptiness" that
Schechner says *is* the stage. Her feelings, then, occupy a spot on the
continuum (albeit an unnameable one) that is nevertheless between the
points of pleasure and pain. We can sense the theatricality of s/m—
the heightening of the poetic "pregnant pause"—and acknowledge that
s/m is a rite of passage for Erica between the world that is overwhelmed
by power and the world that parodies that power. Of course, the passage is never made. There is no end reached, for then Erica would really
become a masochist, wanting to be hurt in everyday life, crossing the
boundary between Lucy's sexual s/m and the "real-life" emotional s/m.

On the contrary, what is reached is a *release* of that power struggle,
a way to "unblock energy" and to encourage trust, honesty, and intimacy (Farr 188). Erica, the masochist in my text, "can no longer do as
she wishes, and thus is completely free." The sadists, here Alexandra
and Vicky, "can do as [they] wish and thus [are] completely free" (Farr
190). Through acting like a masochist, Erica employs Stanislavski's
"magic if" of " 'I am I; but if I were an old oak, set in certain surrounding conditions, what would I do?' " (61). Erica thus becomes,
through the trust of performing fantasies, more "real" to her lovers.
Susan Farr compares this to the process of becoming Real as portrayed in *The Velveteen Rabbit*. As the Skin Horse says: "When you are
Real, you don't mind being hurt. . . . It doesn't happen all at once. You
become. It takes a long time. That's why it doesn't often happen to
people who break easily, or have sharp edges, or who have to be kept.
. . . [O]nce you are Real, you can't be ugly, except to people who don't
understand" (190). This is not unlike the transcendence of performance,
of becoming more real by acting, by imagining; nor is it far from drama
therapy, which specifically uses the mode of drama to solve psychological
problems.

If, however, sadomasochism is only imagining or even a parody of the
gendered power roles, then is it not open to the same criticism as other
performance? As a performance lesbian s/m can be seen as Schechner's
"personal or social interaction" and hence is responsible, as are other
performances, for its representation of lesbians, or of women, or, if ap-
plicable, for its portrayal of African American women, and so on (296).

As feminist critics, we must then ask, "What is the meaning produced by s/m? Who really has the power of subject for which Sue-Ellen Case, among other feminist theatre critics, strives. Is it the sadist or the masochist? (Case 115).

If we return to Jeanie Forte's claim of the power of subversion to make women subjects, then perhaps the answer is both, for both top and bottom have discussed and consented to sadomasochistic sex. Therefore, they are both, in Forte's words, asserting their own pleasure and sexuality, thus denying the fetishistic pursuit to the point of creating a genuine threat to male hegemonic structures of women (263). Of course, things are considerably simplified by the fact that the text in question is one of lesbian s/m. The roles of subject and object get more confusing when examining heterosexual s/m, in which gender is entangled with power and the question of "real" consent. Certainly the actors in Erica's scene were informed by the culture's larger values, but their scene was not burdened with the extra baggage of female and male gender constructions.

In her examination of textual meanings, Sue-Ellen Case offers a startling (though heterosexually defined) analysis of canonized theatre in sadomasochistic terms. Case quotes film critic Laura Mulvey as saying that "the relationship of protagonist and antagonist is sado-masochistic" (124). Here we seem to have come full circle, employing s/m as a way to analyze theatre in itself. The performance of protagonist and antagonist literally becomes Schechner's "personal or social interaction" of s/m sex.

This analysis is locked into the popular conception of man as sadist and woman as masochist. A narrative that can be analyzed this way, Teresa de Lauretis argues, "joins in the reification of male and female sexuality as a battle in which the female is defeated" (quoted in Case 124). This application of the binary of s/m as a means of analyzing texts for phallocentric power is useful as long as the terms *sadist* and *masochist* remain symbols. As seen within the debate over s/m, however, this is not always the case. The s/m of classic protagonist and antagonist is the "emotional S/M" that Lucy distinguishes from "sexual S/M." Without this distinction sadomasochism becomes violent, particularly to women, and then is seen as antifeminist.

However, with the differentiation between the two sides of the mirror, of deciding to perform the role of masochist and of acting masochistic, s/m can be used in feminist politics. By exercising sexual control Erica can choose to play bottom for a night of s/m ritual, thus transcending the constructs of power as negative. Thereby, she can trace the pattern and fascination of woman as masochist in our history but also remain capable of subverting that fetishism by owning it and actively choosing to, as she eloquently said, "get the shit knocked out of [her]." This is what Carole Vance coined "the juxtaposition of pleasure and danger" (1). In this phrase Vance dances between the protectionist (antiporn) and expansionist (pro-sex) sides of feminism, advocating that "women are sexual subjects, sexual actors, sexual agents" (24). Returning to performance theory as Schechner's "double two-way mirror," then, Vance seems to embrace the entire mirror, legitimizing both sides.

This argument of s/m as rebel sex, as guerrilla theatre, is precisely the argument that many pro-s/m lesbians have claimed as justification for their much-questioned sex life. As Pat Califia smirks, "S/M is a deliberate, premeditated, erotic blasphemy" (1979, 19). Even the first sentence in Samois's collection of pro-s/m works reads, "[T]his is an outrageous book" (Davis 7). If, however, sadomasochism is simply fantasy, and if, as Califia argues, "the roles, dialogue, fetish costumes, and sexual activity are part of a drama or ritual" (1979, 21), then why is s/m still so feared and hated? Katherine Davis offers a partial answer to this query when she points out that "what we fear we try to keep contained" (7). The question thus arises: what is it that is so fearful about lesbian s/m? Is it simply that their sex cannot be contained?

That questions of boundaries and containment surface in response to questions of anxiety is hardly surprising, given recent debate over the validity of nonfiction or autobiography in performance. Our trepidation regarding s/m is, I believe, linked to a wider context of anxiety about the Real within the Performed, and it is precisely in this light that the link between antiporn feminists and critiques of s/m becomes most productive. Although we might easily be convinced of the theatricality of sadomasochism, we cannot deny that the spanking, the restraining, the action of this sexual playacting leaves visible scars (the Real). After the mask of "top" or "bottom" has been shed, the body retains the marks of the s/m acts. Sadomasochistic acts in performance art face the same threat of disrupting the actor's body. For example, when New York performer Ron Athey's HIV-positive blood spills from his "performed" piercings, we cannot escape the Reality of his art.

The infringement of the Real within the Performed suggests one explanation for our simultaneous repulsion and fascination with acts of violence on the stage. The tension between the Real and the Performed, recently re-ignited by the flurry of editorials following Arlene Croce's 1994 "review" of Bill T. Jones's *Still/Here,* is an issue of historical weight and significance. In Ancient Greece violence was probably avoided on the stage, because (scholars speculate) of the festival context, audience sensitivities, and/or the presumed three-actor rule. When the

Romans expanded their theatrical repertory to focus on popular enter-tainments and bloodsports, violence became a central part of the (para)-theatrical experience. Still, scholars suspect that Seneca's gory tragedies were not publicly staged, and in both Classical contexts there were vocal outcries against theatre's ability to inflame the passions. Tertullian, writ-ing in the late second century, complains that "there is no spectacle without violent agitation of the soul," expressing an anxiety that resur-faces time and again throughout western theatre's history (Carlson 28). In the eighteenth century Denis Diderot reclaimed these Platonic con-cerns when he stressed the importance of artifice in his *Encyclopedia* entry, *Illusion*. According to Diderot, "total illusion would be revolting or painfully distressing" (289). Violence on the stage, in its threat to the Real human bodies who participate in the Performance, threatens the mimetic paradigm, and it is this exact threat that offers transforma-tive possibilities.

Lesbian sadomasochism, in its irreverent nonproductivity and its fo-cus on pleasure rather than procreation, is an ideal site for challenging age-old taboos regarding not only codes of performance but codes of sexuality as well. The acceptance of lesbian s/m as a private sexual per-formance and sadomasochistic ritual as part of a public performance allows us to examine the generative political potential of enacted plays of power. If, on the other hand, we are ruled by our fear of the Real invading the Performed, the result may be censorship of consensual, premeditated sexually transgressive acts. In this context all would do well to heed Betty Friedan's reminder that "any censorship measure is extremely dangerous to the rights of women as well as men to speak and think freely and to fight for our basic rights, to control our lives, our bodies, and have some degree of economic and political equality" (24). This stance is that of a radical pluralist, accepting diversity, escaping absolutist biological determinism, and "refus[ing] to refuse the body any more" (Weeks 245).

Acknowledgment. The author would like to thank Tracy Davis, Margaret Thompson Drewal, and Alexandra Owen for their guidance on the earliest drafts of this essay, and Mark Pizzato for his assistance on and suggestions for revision.

Works Cited

Brockett, Oscar G. 1996. *The Essential Theatre*. Fort Worth, Tex.: Harcourt.
Califia, Pat. 1979. "A Secret Side of Lesbian Sexuality." *Advocate,* 27 December, 19–23.

———. 1980. "Califia: anti-antiporn." *off our backs* 10 (October): 25.

———. 1981. "Feminism and Sadomasochism." *Heresies* 12:30–34.

Carlson, Marvin. 1984. *Theories of the Theatre*. Ithaca: Cornell University Press.

Case, Sue-Ellen. 1988. *Feminism and Theatre*. New York: Methuen.

Croce, Arlene. 1994–95. "Discussing the Undiscussable." *New Yorker,* 26 December, 54–60.

Davis, Katherine. 1987. "Introduction: What We Fear We Try to Keep Contained." In *Coming to Power: Writings and Graphics on Lesbian S/M.* 7–12. Samois. Boston: Alyson Publications.

Dejanikus, Tacie. 1980. "our legacy." *off our backs* 10 (November): 17, 25.

Diderot, Denis. 1974. "Illusion." *Encyclopedia. Dramatic Theory and Criticism,* ed. Bernard F. Dukore. New York: Holt.

Erica. 1993. Interview. 2 March.

Farr, Susan. 1987. "The Art of Discipline: Creating Erotic Dramas of Play and Power." In *Coming to Power: Writings and Graphics on Lesbian S/M.* 183–90. Samois. Boston: Alyson Publications.

Forte, Jeanie. 1988. "Women's Performance Art: Feminism and Postmodernism." *Theatre Journal* 40 (May): 251–69.

Friedan, Betty. 1987. "Feminism." *The Meese Commission Exposed.* Ed. National Coalition Against Censorship. 2d ed. New York: NCAC. 30–34.

Lucy, Juicy. 1987. "If I Ask You to Tie Me Up, Will You Still Want to Love Me?" In *Coming to Power: Writings and Graphics on Lesbian S/M.* 29–40. Samois. Boston: Alyson Publications.

Rich, Adrienne. 1989. "Compulsory Heterosexuality and Lesbian Existence." In *Feminist Frontiers II,* ed. Laurel Richardson and Verta Taylor. 2d ed. New York: McGraw.

Samois. 1987. *Coming to Power: Writings and Graphics on Lesbian S/M.* Boston: Alyson Publications.

Schechner, Richard. 1985. *Between Theater and Anthropology.* Philadelphia: Pennsylvania University Press.

Stanislavski, Constantin. 1984. *An Actor Prepares.* New York: Theatre Arts.

Vance, Carole S. 1984. "Pleasure and Danger: Towards a Politics of Sexuality." In *Pleasure and Danger.* New York: Routledge.

Weeks, Jeffrey. 1986. *Sexuality and Its Discontents: Meanings, Myths, and Modern Sexualities.* London: Routledge.

Zawinski, Andrea, ed. 1980. "lesbians and pornography." *off our backs* 10 (July): 9.

Violence at the Royal Court

Martin McDonagh's *The Beauty Queen of Leenane* and Mark Ravenhill's *Shopping and Fucking*

William C. Boles

> "I've figured out a way where it will appear that a cat is being blown up. It isn't, really, but the audience will believe that it is. I think it makes some people uncomfortable."
>
> —Martin McDonagh musing on why his play
> *The Lieutenant of Inishmore* is still unproduced (Lyman 19).

EXPLODING CATS AND UNCOMFORTABLE AUDIENCES. Welcome to the second renaissance of contemporary English drama, which is always surprising, ever challenging and, on occasion, a tad messy. Gone from their comfortable (but by now timeworn) chairs of drama are John Osborne and his Angry Young Writer colleagues. In their places are a number of hip, twenty-to-thirty-something, Quentin Tarantino–influenced movie lovers who are visually driven, verbally profane, violently articulate, and sexually precocious. They are the New Brutalists.[1] Some of the playwrights (and plays) that belong to this, the hottest new club in England, are Jez Butterworth (*Mojo*, 1995); Sarah Kane (*Blasted*, 1995); Jim Cartwright (*I Licked a Slag's Deodorant*, 1996); Patrick Marber (*Closer*, 1997); Doug Lucie (*The Shallow End*, 1997); and Joe Penhall (*Truth and Understanding*, 1997). However, the two playwrights and plays receiving most of the attention are Martin McDonagh and his *Beauty Queen of Leenane* (1996) and Mark Ravenhill and his *Shopping and Fucking* (1996).

Although the New Brutalists may share the same frank critical atti-

---

[1]Some critics have also dubbed them the New Nihilists.

tude about the state of Great Britain as their predecessors, their method of presentation and motives for writing differ markedly. Rather than espousing a heavy-handed, leftist critique of the country's problems, the New Brutalists strive instead to elicit visceral responses from their audiences (hence the exploding cat) by graphically depicting the harrowing lives of their characters.[2] They are equally engaged in portraying (often in scatological terms) the lives of oppressed, disenfranchised individuals, many of them youths, in the midst of struggles in a comfortless and vapid world and their attempts to escape never-ending boredom through drugs, sex, money, stories, microwave dinners, innocuous television programs and/or violence. It is precisely this latter element—violence—in both plays that is the subject of this article.

With the exception of the Royal Shakespeare Company's 1993 production of *King Lear,* no production has made me consciously aware of my own physical, emotional, and intellectual reactions to violence being enacted on a stage. In January of 1997, however, when I took a group of twenty students to see the Royal Court's productions of *The Beauty Queen of Leenane* and *Shopping and Fucking,* I found myself at the plays' violent conclusions once again experiencing the same reactions—shock, disgust, nausea, and a great sense of discomfort—that I had had at witnessing the blinding of Gloucester. Throughout the rest of our stay in London my students and I maintained a running discussion of the plays and their violent endings. Was the violence onstage merely gratuitous and there for the sake of making the audience uncomfortable, as McDonagh had suggested in this article's epigraph? Or was there something more to the violence? We never really reached fully satisfying answers before leaving England.

My purpose in this article is therefore to "return" to these plays a year later in order to reexamine the violence in those scenes that have embedded themselves permanently in my theatrical memory. It is my contention that their violence is clearly not gratuitous, primarily because both playwrights successfully fuse violence with the hypnotic and curative powers of storytelling. In effect, McDonagh uses violence to disrupt

---

[2]Documentation of these visceral reactions can be found principally in the London reviews of *Shopping and Fucking,* in which the critics continually remark on the physical cuffing they received while watching the play. Jack Tinker of the *Daily Mail,* for example, felt like the play hit him "like a punch in the solar plexus—or even lower below the belt" (50). John Peter of the *Sunday Times* admits: "There is a scene of homosexual sex that, for the first time in my life, gave me a sense of real physical nausea in the theatre," but he then adds, "and yet I can see that without such scenes the play would not pack the moral punch it does" (14).

the spell of storytelling, whereas Ravenhill uses it as a means of "making" a story come true.

As critics have already noted, the setting and structure of *Beauty Queen* are hardly new to the stage. The Irish countryside recalls any number of Irish plays, most notably Synge's bucolic *Playboy of the Western World,* and the well-made play scheme (with its clichéd reliance on a letter) has served as the structure for dramas as substantial as Ibsen's *A Doll's House.* Equally, the plot is fairly conventional, with Maureen, the dutiful but embittered daughter, whiling away her life caring for Mag, her aging, cantankerous, and shrewish mother, while awaiting her opportunity to escape. All this admittedly is fairly conventional, yet to these familiar elements McDonagh has added a sinister trace of menace and brutality. At times in the play it almost seems as if Pinter, Bond, Mamet, Synge, and Ibsen had collaborated on a play, with *Beauty Queen* the result.

The play's brutality is nowhere more evident than in a scene near the end, when Maureen finally has the opportunity to leave the stultifying Irish countryside and go to Boston with her lover, Pato. Maureen's plans are thwarted when Mag intercepts the letter containing Pato's proposal, reads it, and then burns it. Maureen discovers her mother's deviousness just as Pato is leaving for the United States and extracts her revenge, which is accomplished in the following manner:

> Maureen stares at [Mag] in dumb shock and hate, then walks to the kitchen, dazed, puts a chip-pan on the stove, turns it on high and pours a half-bottle of cooking oil into it. . . . Maureen slowly and deliberately takes her mother's shriveled hand, holds it down on the burning range, and starts slowly pouring some of the hot oil over it, as Mag screams in pain and terror. . . . Maureen, in a single and almost lazy motion, throws the considerable remainder of the oil into Mag's midriff, some of it splashing up into her face. Mag doubles-up, screaming, falls to the floor, trying to pat the oil off her, and lies there convulsing, screaming and whimpering while Maureen then rushes to the train station to intercept Pato (46–48).

In the next scene Maureen is discovered prowling around the room and brandishing a fireplace poker as she describes her farewell meeting with Pato, during which she promised to go to him as soon as she could find someone to take care of her mother. Mag sits silently in her chair, rocking. The scene ends as the chair stops rocking and Mag tumbles out of it. "A red chunk of skull hangs from a string of skin at the side of [Mag's] head" (51).

Not surprisingly, Maureen's treatment of Mag shocks the audience. At the performance I attended, in fact, the entire audience gasped audibly when Maureen poured the burning oil on her mother's hand. Through observable action, McDonagh clearly establishes the violent nature of the environment, a violence he then reinforces through the characters' dialogue, which is loaded with references to brutality. For example, when Ray (Pato's brother) first visits Mag and Maureen, he and Mag talk about a priest hitting a youth in the head "and for no reason." Ray tries to justify the act to Mag: "Father Welsh seldom uses violence, same as most young priests. It's usually only the older priests go punching you in the head" (9). In another scene Maureen and Pato talk about a man who cut off his brother's dog's ears. And later Ray waxes excitedly about a poker (the same one that Maureen will use later to kill Mag): "This is a great oul poker, . . . Good and heavy and long. A half a dozen coppers you could take out with this poker and barely notice and have not a scratch on it and then clobber them again just for the fun of seeing the blood running out of them" (39). These and other passages from the text clearly demonstrate that violence is a regular component of the characters' daily existence, and these examples, although operating in the dramatic present, also serve to foreshadow the violence to come.

However, what is so evident on the printed page—the palpable presence of violence—is almost totally lost when the play is translated to the stage, for in the theatre *Beauty Queen* is hysterically funny. This "strange" humor is demonstrated in the following conversation between Mag and Maureen, in which Mag tells Maureen about a murderer in Dublin:

MAUREEN: Sure, that sounds exactly the type of fella I would *like* to meet, and bring him home to meet you, if he likes murdering oul women. . . .

MAG: (pause) Sure why would he be coming all this way out from Dublin? He'd just be going out of his way.

MAUREEN: For the pleasure of me company he'd come. Killing you, it'd just be a bonus for him.

MAG: Killing *you* I bet he first would be.

MAUREEN: I could live with that so long as I was sure he'd be clobbering you soon after. If he clobbered you with a big axe or something and took your ould head off and spat in your neck, I wouldn't mind at all, going first. Oh ho, I'd enjoy it, I would (6).

The audience laughs at the seeming playfulness of this exchange because it recognizes the playwright's uncanny ability to capture the essence of the everyday cruelties we practice and because of the richly textured and humorous characters he has created.[3] And it is largely because of the humor of the play in production that the violence at the play's end is a surprise, for in truth McDonagh has fooled his audience. He has made it think that it was watching a comedy, when actually the piece was considerably darker, more vicious. As the violent and rather shocking exchanges take place, spectators, engrossed in laughter, miss the sinister overtones of these conversations and as a consequence never consider them as seriously as they should.

This bit of "misdirection" is typical of McDonagh's attitude toward and his use of his audience. He has admitted to enjoying the shock spectators encounter at seeing one of his plays, declaring, "[T]here are times when people in the audiences are hit with bits of stuff flying off the stage. . . . I love to be in the theatre and watch that. The people in the audience jump out of their skins. I don't know why I love it. I think it's a power thing, really" (Lyman 19). McDonagh's manipulation of his audience manifests itself in the portrayal of the daily battles between Mag and Maureen in which he forces each audience member to take a position. Does the spectator sympathize with the ailing and mistreated but conniving, annoying, selfish mother who only wants her daughter to stay with her? Or does the viewer sympathize with the seemingly dutiful, hardworking, but mean-spirited daughter who has never had a beau? In the first act McDonagh makes such a decision impossible by endowing both characters with sympathetic, as well as damning, qualities.

However, in the beginning of the second act McDonagh deftly sways the audience to one character's side. The act opens on the morning after Pato and Maureen have spent the night together. While he makes breakfast for Mag, Maureen, wearing only a slip, flaunts her night of passion with Pato before her mother: "You'll have to be putting that thing of yours in me again before too long is past, Pato. I do have a taste for it now, I do" (28). Jealous and angry about her daughter's change of fortune, Mag strikes back, telling Pato: "She's the one that scoulded me hand! I'll tell you that, now! . . . Held it down on the range she did! Poured chip-pan fat o'er it! Aye, and told the doctor it was me!" (28). Maureen, unconcerned by her mother's accusation, counters by saying

---

[3]Sarah Hemming writes: "He is wonderful at capturing the mean little acts whereby people torment one another" (21); and Charles Spencer observes: "The relationship [between Mag and Maureen] is charted with the blackest of humour, and the baleful silences, festering resentments and moments of virulent spite are all wickedly enjoyable" (23).

that Mag is senile, and to prove it she has Pato smell the kitchen sink, which reeks of urine. She tells Pato that every morning Mag pours the contents of her bed pan down the sink—an image from which the audience invariably recoils.

It is at this moment that both the audience and Pato make a decision about which character to believe and begin to answer questions—Is Mag truly a vengeful, vindictive old woman bent on destroying any hint of happiness in her daughter's life? Or is Maureen, as Mag suggests, violently abusive?—that McDonagh raised earlier in the play. Through this scene McDonagh makes it easy for the audience to choose between the characters. Like Pato, the audience automatically sides with Maureen, for no physical action in the play to this point supports Mag's allegations of her daughter's brutality; whereas Mag's cruelty, symbolized by her burning Pato's proposal, as well as her seemingly senile mannerisms—her repeated, simplistic questions and sedentary position before the television—seem to support Maureen's contention. So even though Mag tells the truth, she becomes the villain, whereas Maureen lies and becomes the sympathetic victim.

It is my contention, then, that much of the shock at the scenes of violence is derived not as much from the horrific torture on stage (although it is quite realistic) as from the spectator's realization that McDonagh has cleverly deceived them both into thinking the play was a comedy and also into sympathizing with a parent-abuser and murderer, while hating the victim. When we are duped, it alerts us to the fact that perhaps we are not quite as savvy as we thought we were. The violent ending, then, becomes not only a physical attack against Mag but also a violent shock to our own theatre-going sensibilities. Through his dramaturgy McDonagh reawakens our appreciation of the power of the well-made play and its ability to succeed on the contemporary stage.

Whereas *Beauty Queen* takes place in the picturesque countryside of Ireland and suggests parallels to Synge and Ibsen, Ravenhill's *Shopping and Fucking* explores the nightclubs, stores, arcades, and seedy flats of London and recalls Irvine Welsh's *Trainspotting,* which was a popular novel before becoming a play and then a movie. Mimi Kramer accurately described *Shopping and Fucking* as belonging to "the subgenre of so-called smack-and-sodomy plays, in which drug use is rampant and sex is graphic, brutish and usually anal" (71–72). And the play's final violent scene is precisely that: "graphic, brutish and anal."

In *Shopping and Fucking* a fourteen-year-old rent boy named Gary seeks the fulfillment of his fantasy, which is to be sodomized by a father figure. He offers Robbie, a failed Ecstasy drug dealer who owes his supplier money, £1000 to perform the act. Robbie sodomizes Gary, and then Mark, Robbie's former lover and Gary's current "involvement," takes his place. As he has intercourse with Gary, Mark slams the youth's head against the tabletop and repeatedly pummels him. Lulu, Robbie's lover, who has been watching the scene, stops the beating, but Gary demands that they continue. However, the story he wants reenacted is not accurately being rendered.

> GARY: My story doesn't end like this. He doesn't just fuck me. . . . Because in the story he's always got something. It depends, changes. He gets me in the room, ties me up. But he doesn't just wanna fuck me does he? Cos it's not him, it's not his dick, it's a knife. He fucks me with a knife.
>
> So..(Pause)
>
> Gotta have something.
>
> Everybody's got something. The kitchen. Or, or a screwdriver. Or something. . . . Got to be fucking something. That's how the story ends. (83–84)

Ultimately, Mark sodomizes Gary offstage with a fork, killing the boy.

Unlike McDonagh's play, which through its comedy initially shields the spectator somewhat from the underlying violence of the work, Ravenhill's drama deliberately and graphically depicts an English society awash in violence, anarchy, sexual abuse, drug use, oppression, and predatory relationships. Numerous scenes in the first act establish the dire situation of this society. Mark rejects an offer of food from Lulu and then vomits on stage; an unconcerned Lulu, reciting Chekhov, auditions topless for Brian, a drug dealer; Robbie is beaten after a botched attempt to sell Ecstasy at a nightclub; Lulu witnesses a horrific stabbing at the 7-11, but instead of helping the victim, she steals a chocolate bar (another customer steals a *TV Guide*); Mark pays to lick Gary's anus, only to find his mouth covered with blood. This last scene is particularly telling of the play's horrific environment, as Gary explains to Mark in the following speech that he is bleeding because his stepfather raped him repeatedly:

> GARY: I went to the council. And I said to her, 'Look, it's simple: he's fucking me. Once, twice, three times a week he comes into my room. He's a big man. He holds me down and he fucks me.' . . . and she says 'Does he use a condom?' . . . I tell her he's fucking me—without a condom—and she says to me—you know what she says? . . . 'I think I've got a leaflet. Would you like to give him a leaflet?' (39–40).

Not only have the characters and the government become inured to the brutality of the violence around them, but communal, self-affirming personal relationships have disappeared as well. Emotional relationships are devoid of commitment, love, trust, and respect, having been replaced by transactions. Money drives these characters, as Brian "lectures" Robbie: "Money is civilization" (87).

To avoid the vapid world around them and to fill the voids in their lives the characters create stories that provide justification for their existence. Robbie, Lulu, and Mark, for example, ritualistically retell, reshape, and remodel the story of how they came to be a family. They also make up stories about the most famous person with whom they have had intercourse.[4] In one of the play's funniest and best-written scenes Lulu and Robbie attempt to raise the £3000 in drug money they owe Brian by setting up a phone-sex hot line, through which they fulfill the fantasies of or create stories for their paying callers.

Throughout, Ravenhill refuses to allow the audience to separate itself from the characters' obsession with storytelling. In one scene he draws us into the play's world by having Brian retell (in a slightly misquoted form) one of the most successful stories of the 1990s, Walt Disney's *The Lion King*, relating to Lulu the most touching part of the story for him and his son:

BRIAN: So now the father is dead. Murdered. It was the uncle. And the son has grown up. . . . And this sort of monkey thing comes to him. And this monkey says: "It's time to speak to your dead dad." So he goes to the stream and he looks in and he sees his own reflection. . . . But then . . . the water ripples, it hazes. Until he sees a ghost. A ghost or a memory looking up at him. His . . . (Pause.) Excuse me. It takes you right there. Your throat tightens. Until . . . he sees . . . his . . . dad.

My little one. Gets to that bit and I look round and he's got these big tears in his eyes. He feels it like I do.

Because now the dad speaks. And he says: "The time has come. It is time for you to take your place in the Cycle of Being (words to that effect). You are my son and the one true King."

And he knows what it is he's got to do. He knows who it is he has to kill.

And that's the moment. That's our favorite bit. (7)

Brian's retelling of the story stresses the father-son bond of familial obligation, emotional attachment, and cyclical regeneration not only

---

[4]Mark tells a hysterical story about a fictional sexual encounter in a bathroom stall with Princesses Di and Fergie, both dressed in police uniforms.

for Brian and his son but for the story's two main characters as well. Ravenhill includes this story precisely because it is the antithesis of the reality of the situation in which the characters live. Brian rhapsodizes over his son, at the same time asking Lulu to take off her shirt and giving her three hundred Ecstasy pills. Rather than spending time with his child, Brian carries a videotaped performance of his son's recital in his briefcase (along with a videotape of Lulu's topless performance). For Brian, just like the other characters, the story of the lion king makes him believe he is part of the ideal father-son relationship simply because he and his son both enjoy the same story.

Even more telling is Gary's desire to have a father, which Ravenhill also projects through the lion king story. As Gary tells Mark, "I want a dad. I want someone to look after me. I want someone so strong that when he holds me in his arms the world can't get to me. And I want him to fuck me. . . . And yeah, it'll hurt. But a good hurt" (31). Unlike *The Lion King,* in which the son avenges the death of the father and restores a proper sense of order to the kingdom, Gary's fantasy negates the father-son alliance by his seeking a father figure who will kill him. The son becomes the victim of the father rather than his redeemer. In essence, where Brian's version focuses on the cyclical nature of father-son relationships, Gary and the world in which he lives foster a need to halt the "Cycle of Being." As the father figure in Gary's story engages in a nonreproductive sexual act with his own son and then slays him, he nullifies the very notions of family, human progress, inheritance, and regeneration. Ironically, in the process he also prevents future generations from struggling through such a hellish existence.

And yet in both stories the violence is generated out of a sense of love and obligation. As Gary tells Mark, "I want you to do it. Come on. You can do it. . . . I've been looking. Looking and I can't find him. . . . He hasn't got a face in the story. He's in my head—waiting—but. I want to put a face to him. Your face. Do it. Do it and I'll say 'I love you'" (85).

Following Gary's murder, the world that had seemed so askew rights itself once again, just as the young cub's killing of his uncle restores order to that world. Ravenhill, then, relies on our own pop-culture fascination with *The Lion King* in order to draw connections between his theatrical world and our own. In this context his violent ending ultimately serves the same purpose as the violence at the end of the Disney movie. Through Gary's murder, love, albeit brief and unregenerative, is finally achieved.

The endings of *Shopping and Fucking* and *The Beauty Queen of Leenane* posit two different attitudes toward violence and the results of violence. In *Shopping and Fucking* the murder of Gary would seem to be just another brutal crime among brutal crimes. However, his death has the effect of cleansing his world, and the play ends optimistically as Brian tells Lulu, Robbie, and Mark about the end of *The Lion King*, when the son holds the new cub up toward the sky for his father to see, a striking contrast to the fate of Gary. Mark then retells the story of Lulu, Robbie, and his family by setting it in the future with a different, more optimistic ending and a promise of freedom. And finally, the play ends where it began, with Mark, Robbie, and Lulu eating microwave dinners. In this case, though, Mark does not vomit. Instead, the characters eat their meals (something they have been unable to do the entire play) and feed each other as the lights come down. Thus, Ravenhill suggests that finally a time of nourishment, companionship, and love has arrived. Ironically, and perhaps a bit cynically, the violent murder, the death of the child, has drawn them together and made them a stronger family.

Whereas Ravenhill seemingly condones the murder of Gary, McDonagh refuses to allow Maureen to escape unpunished. As she prepares to leave for Boston she learns that Pato is about to get married.[5] At the news Maureen physically metamorphoses into her mother, sitting in her mother's rocking chair, repeating the same phrases her mother uttered, and even eating the same foods. However, unlike Mag, Maureen has no one to care for her, and consequently she will live the remainder of her life by herself. Ultimately, her act of violence has condemned her to a life alone. In essence, McDonagh, for all of his postmodern interest in shocking and surprising the audience, still clings to some notion of poetic justice.

In 1965 the premiere of Edward Bond's *Saved* provoked outrage and protest because of a scene portraying a group of youths stoning an infant to death. Thirty years later *Saved* is considered one of the most important plays to emerge not only from one of the Angry Young writers of the sixties but also from a British playwright in the twentieth century. Although the stoning of the baby is still a brutal and haunting depiction of the violence of which humans are capable, the play's critical reputation has moved beyond the controversy surrounding that one scene.

Currently, the type of vituperative outrage that surrounded the opening of *Saved* is strangely missing from reactions to *The Beauty Queen of Leenane* and *Shopping and Fucking*. And yet the same questions about

---

[5]Evidently, on the night of her mother's murder, Maureen never actually saw Pato at the train station. She mistook another man for him.

the necessity of, as well as the graphic representations of, violence on stage that plagued Bond's work still linger over these two works and those of fellow New Brutalists. For the time being, then, McDonagh and Ravenhill will have to wait to see if their own works, like Bond's, will evoke the horror necessary to focus attention on humankind's brutality and will, like Bond's masterwork, become "resonating documents" about the state of the United Kingdom and the end of the twentieth century.

Works Cited

Hemming, Sarah. 1996. Review of *The Beauty Queen of Leenane*. *Financial Times*, 12 March, 21.

Kramer, Mimi. 1997. "Three for the Show." *Time*, 4 August, 71–72.

Lyman, Rick. 1998. "Most Promising (and Grating) Playwright." *New York Times Magazine*, 25 January, 16–19.

McDonagh, Martin. 1996. *The Beauty Queen of Leenane*. London: Methuen.

Peter, John. 1996. Review of *Shopping and Fucking*. *Sunday Times* (London), 6 October, sec. 10, p. 14.

Ravenhill, Mark. 1996. *Shopping and Fucking*. London: Methuen.

Spencer, Charles. 1996. Review of *The Beauty Queen of Leenane*. *Daily Telegraph*, 8 March, 23.

Tinker, Jack. 1996. Review of *Shopping and Fucking*. *Daily Mail*, 4 October, 50.

Contributors

Jane Barnette received a B.S. degree in Theatre and Women's Studies at Northwestern University and is currently entering candidacy for the Ph.D. degree in Theatre History and Criticism at the University of Texas, where she also teaches a survey theatre course and works for *Theatre Insight*.

William C. Boles is Assistant Professor of English at Rollins College. He has published a number of articles on Contemporary British Drama, including a forthcoming chapter for a Wendy Wasserstein casebook that relates Wasserstein to Caryl Churchill and Charlotte Keatley.

John C. Countryman is Associate Professor and Director of Theatre at Berry College. He has written a number of papers and articles on the works of Brian Friel and Belfast playwright, John Boyd. Dr. Countryman has traveled extensively in the Republic of Ireland and Northern Ireland and is currently working on a critical biography of Boyd.

Lesley Ferris is Chair of the Department of Theatre at The Ohio State University and former Chair of the Department of Theatre at Louisiana State University. She is an experienced director and writer and received an Arts Council of Great Britain playwriting grant for her script *Subjugation of the Dragon*. She has published numerous articles and two books: *Acting Women: Images of Women in Theatre* and *Crossing the Stage: Controversies on Cross Dressing*.

Dale Anthony Girard is an award-winning Fight Director, one of only eleven recognized Fight Masters in the United States, and the author of the stage combat manual *Actors On Guard*. His work has been featured in professional theatres and opera houses throughout North America and in several feature films. He is currently Stage Combat Instructor at the Yale School of Drama.

James Harley is a doctoral student in Theatre History and Criticism at the University of Texas-Austin, where he teaches introductory theatre subjects. His article "The Theatre of Death: The Theatrical Elaboration of Ancient Roman Blood Spectacles" has recently been published in *Theatre History Studies*.

Charlotte Headrick is Professor of Theatre Arts and Assistant Chair of the Department of Speech Communication at Oregon State University. She is a past recipient of the Kennedy Center Medallion and a former Elizabeth P. Ritchie Distinguished Professor at Oregon State. Dr. Headrick's specialty is Irish women playwrights, and she has published a number of articles on the subject.

Colleen Kelly is Resident Fight Director and Associate Director of the Professional Actor Training Program at the Alabama Shakespeare Festival. She is Vice President of the Society of American Fight Directors and has presented lectures on theatrical swordplay at the international Stage Combat Workshop in London and for the Folger Library's exhibition, "The Sword and the Pen."

J. D. Martinez is Associate Professor of Theatre at Washington & Lee University. Mr. Martinez is an internationally recognized Master of the Stage Combat Arts and past President of the Society of American Fight Directors. He is the author of *Combat Mime, a Non-Violent Approach to Stage Violence,* and *The Swords of Shakespeare, an Illustrated Guide to Stage Combat Choreography in the Plays of Shakespeare.* He is currently working on a book titled *Violence as Entertainment.*

Andrea J. Nouryeh is Associate Professor of Dramatic Literature and Theatre History at St. Lawrence University, where she serves as Resident Dramaturg for the Department of Speech and Theatre. She is coauthor of an anthology, *Drama and Performance,* and a contributor to two reference books: *Theatrical Designers* and *Theatre Directors: A Biographical Dictionary.* Since 1994 she has served as a member and then President of the Board of CAVA, a nonprofit agency in St. Lawrence county that counsels victims of sexual assault and domestic violence.

Nancy Scheper-Hughes is Chair of the Department of Anthropology and Professor of Anthropology at the University of California-Berkeley. She is a past recipient of a Fulbright Scholar Award, a John Simon Guggenheim Award, and two Harry Frank Guggenheim Foundation grants. Dr. Scheper-Hughes has authored, edited, and/or coedited five books; contributed numerous articles and chapters to books and scholarly journals; delivered over fifty conference papers; organized dozens of special conference sessions and symposia; and lectured widely in this country and abroad.

Leslie A. Wade is Associate Professor of Dramatic Literature, Theory and Criticism at Louisiana State University. His book, *Sam Shepard and the American Theatre,* was published in 1997, and he has published essays in numerous books and journals. Professor Wade is also a playwright and a recent recipient of the Louisiana State Art Council's fellowship in playwriting. His works have won awards from the Association for Theatre in Higher Education, the Los Angeles Arts Council, and the American College Theatre Festival.